What people are saying about …

THOU SHALT NOT BE A JERK

"Poll after poll has shown that the involvement of Christians in divisive politics has deeply damaged the witness of the church in America. Eugene Cho has given us an important wake-up call—reminding us that our most powerful witness is not found in politics, but in the moral and spiritual power of the gospel of Jesus Christ."

Richard Stearns, president emeritus of World Vision US and author of *The Hole in Our Gospel*

"You see, the thing about Eugene Cho is that he's committed to a holistic understanding of the gospel. But his commitment to Jesus is not merely intellectual, it's *actionable*. Whether you lean 'Right' or 'Left' or "in-between' in your political perspective, you will be challenged, encouraged, and equipped by this robust work."

Dr. Derwin L. Gray, founding and lead pastor of Transformation Church and author of The Good Life

"I have been waiting for this book because the Church desperately needs this book more than ever before. So many leaders and believers regularly ask me for wisdom around how to navigate our Christian faith and politics. While this book may not have all the answers, Rev. Eugene Cho has written an incredible and timely resource by providing a biblical, theological, and practical framework to both encourage and challenge pastors, leaders, and all believers. He bravely balances the pastoral and prophetic and urges us not to abandon politics but to faithfully work to ensure that our theology as followers of Jesus informs our politics and not the other way around. Indeed, we need to hear and embody this message!"

Dr. John M. Perkins, founder and president emeritus of John & Vera Mae Perkins Foundation and founder of Christian Community Development Association

"One of the great challenges in the US church today is for Christians to effectively engage in politics without being overtly partisan and to resist the temptation to completely disengage politically because it can be so toxic and wearing. This book provides an essential framework for how Christians can engage in the public square to be salt and light, to demonstrate the love and good news of Christ for all people by engaging the systems and structures in which we live. Choosing to be apolitical is not an option—it's how we engage in politics well that will allow us to fully advance the cause of Christ to a watching and waiting world."

Jenny Yang, vice president of advocacy and policy at World Relief and coauthor of *Welcoming the Stranger*

"How do we engage politically as Christians when our political disagreements have ended friendships, divided families and church communities, and left people bruised, determined to avoid anything political? In *Thou Shall Not Be a Jerk*, Eugene Cho is not reductive about the prayer-filled yet significantly divergent political views Christians hold. But he doesn't give up either. Instead, Cho calls us beyond apathy, avoidance, and echo chambers, equipping Christians to listen and engage politically with humility, integrity, conviction. This book is both challenging and inspiring. And a valuable resource as we seek to navigate a polarized climate with grace and truth."

Jo Saxton, speaker, author, and leadership coach

"Conversations about how Christians should engage with politics have always been difficult, but are needed now more than ever. I'm grateful that Eugene has always strived to approach these questions with a humility to learn and try to first and foremost understand what God would want us to do. I'm still continuing to learn and am grateful for the guidance and insights that this book provides."

Jeremy Lin, professional basketball player and 2019 NBA champion, and founder of Jeremy Lin Foundation

"Eugene has thoughtfully challenged us to engage with politics in the backward way of Jesus, with humility, love, and passion. Goodness, we need a new way to engage our world—and he has challenged us to it."

Jennie Allen, author of *Get Out of Your Head* and founder and visionary of IF:Gathering

"Eugene Cho's tome is a welcome and instructive guide to Christians of every political stripe who in this time of deep political divide are in profound need of a cartography to engage in the political sphere while reflecting their primary allegiance to Christian discipleship and the kingdom of God."

Rev. Dr. Gabriel Salguero, pastor of Calvario City Church and president of National Latino Evangelical Coalition

EUGENE
CHO

THOU SHALT NOT BE A JERK

A Christian's Guide
to Engaging Politics

DAVID C COOK

transforming lives together

THOU SHALT NOT BE A JERK
Published by David C Cook
4050 Lee Vance Drive
Colorado Springs, CO 80918 U.S.A.

Integrity Music Limited, a Division of David C Cook
Brighton, East Sussex BN1 2RE, England

The graphic circle C logo is a registered trademark of David C Cook.

The website addresses recommended throughout this book are offered as a
resource to you. These websites are not intended in any way to be or imply an
endorsement on the part of David C Cook, nor do we vouch for their content.

Details in some stories have been changed to protect
the identities of the persons involved.

Library of Congress Control Number 2019948025
ISBN 978-0-7814-1115-8
eISBN 978-0-8307-7891-1

© 2020 Eugene Cho

The Team: Michael Covington, Alice Crider, Nick Lee,
Megan Stengel, Jack Campbell, Susan Murdock
Cover Design: Jon Middel

Printed in the United States of America
First Edition 2020

1 2 3 4 5 6 7 8 9 10

121319

Family.

To my parents: Thank you for your courage—in fleeing for freedom during the Korean War and later immigrating to the United States so that your children might have opportunities you didn't have in your life.

To my wife, Minhee: I love you and am so grateful to be on this journey of serving and honoring Christ together.

To Jubilee, Trinity, and Jedi: I see you, love you, and believe in you.

CONTENTS

ACKNOWLEDGMENTS

No book is every written alone. Sincere gratitude to so many who worked with me on this book, along with friends and family who kept cheering me on.

Special thanks to Chris, Derek, Cheryl, and Alice, Jack, and the team at David C Cook.

Finally, much love to George, Jin, and Joanie for your steadfast friendship and humbling generosity to my family during this season of our lives.

INTRODUCTION

POLITICS MATTER

Authors might feel compelled to invest their time writing a book for many different reasons. Some might be drawn by a particular excitement or passion, and others might feel a sense of burden. Both are important. As a pastor and leader trying to help guide churches, other leaders, and Christians in our current landscape, it's not excitement that motivates me to write this book. In fact, I never envisioned I would be writing a book about the intersection of faith and politics—especially one entitled *Thou Shalt Not Be a Jerk*. What a downer!

However, I feel *compelled* to write this book. In other words, I am burdened for the church and the aspect of discipleship and Christlikeness that often feels in short supply in our culture. I've even started the first chapters of many other books on more "safe" or "spiritual" topics, but I keep feeling *called* back to this book. I didn't major in political science in college. Nor am I a "politics junkie" or an expert on all things at the intersection of faith and politics. I've never run for public office or served on anyone's campaign; although, I unsuccessfully ran for middle school president (I can still picture the "Vote for

Cho" posters). I have much to learn and there are many other books you can read, which I'll quote and recommend.

So, why write this book?

As I shared, I am deeply concerned and, at times, deeply grieved by the state of the political affairs in our society. Even as I write this book, I'm processing horrific recent news of pipe bombs mailed to political leaders, shootings at Jewish synagogues, a mass shooting at a mosque in New Zealand, and bomb explosions in churches and hotels in Sri Lanka. These terrorist attacks are indeed despicable and should be condemned by everyone. But we should not pretend this happened overnight. The unconscionable is *possible* when, over the years, we've normalized violent rhetoric, mocking, bullying, and the demonization of others. Clearly, we can't blame it merely on the broad umbrella of politics, but it's plain to many that something has significantly shifted in our culture and politics to our detriment.

Within the church, it's all too convenient to blame the larger culture and society. I'm equally concerned by the manner in which Christians are engaging the political machine. For example, certain Christians have altogether dismissed and disengaged themselves from the political process—either because it's too exhausting or because of the theological bent that shapes their conclusion that a follower of Jesus should only focus on "spiritual things." Simultaneously, I'm concerned by Christians who appear to be overly obsessed by politics, and by this I mean we've chosen to justify everything we do for the sake of our political ideologies, views, or convictions. Additionally, I'm concerned by Christians who are heavily influenced by a vision of cultural Christianity and the power we can wield in our society without necessarily being about the ways and heart of Christ.

While many present various great challenges to Christianity, including secularism, I would submit that the greatest challenge is actually *within Christianity*: It's the temptation to build the structures and institutionalism of Christianity but without a parallel commitment to Jesus. It's politicians and even Christian pastors and leaders who sprinkle on a pinch of Jesus into our thinking, speeches, or sermons but often in a way that fulfills our agenda or goals. In other words, using Jesus to promote nationalism is simply not the way of Jesus. This is the danger of *cultural Christianity* that eventually, and predictably, produces cultural Christians rather than disciples of Jesus.

From a political perspective, cultural Christianity is when our theology is held captive by our politics rather than our politics being informed and even transformed by our theology. The danger of this predicament takes us back to the Garden of Eden where Adam and Eve were tempted to be like, or even to be, God. In other words, the oldest sin in humanity has been to conform God into our image. So, as we read the Scriptures, if we're never offended, convicted, disrupted, or stirred by the Holy Spirit, it's quite possible that we've conformed Jesus into our thinking, liking, and ... image.

So, what are the dangers and implications of cultural Christianity? Imagine a Christianity that conforms to a culture—in all of its shifts and changes—and no longer adheres to the scandalous, radical love, grace, teachings, and life of Jesus Christ. Imagine an institutional Christianity that's obsessed with power, influence, and platform without a commitment to the countercultural commitment of Jesus Christ; a commitment to empire rather than the kingdom of God.

How else could we explain what transpired in Germany with the rise of Hitler and Nazism? In Germany, at the start of World War II, some historians report that up to 94 percent of the nation were professing Christians.[1] How could there be such dissonance except to acknowledge the ills and poison of cultural Christianity? How else could we explain why so many would profess to be Christians and yet choose to become seduced by the evil propaganda of Hitler?

But it wasn't just merely an anomaly in Nazi Germany. We have witnessed this throughout history when Christian institutions go to bed with power and then embody practices that are antithetical to the gospel. This was evident when religious leaders used erroneous theology to dismiss and judge the poor in the book of Amos. This was evident when missionaries engaged in horrific practices of colonization and abuse of power with Native American boarding schools. What an incredible stain to the witness of Christ to the world.

During the summer of 2019, I was invited by World Relief to lead a small group of American pastors to travel to Rwanda for the purpose of listening and learning about truth telling, confession, forgiveness, justice, and reconciliation from Rwandan citizens, activists, and pastors. Why Rwanda? Tragically, the people and nation of Rwanda experienced what has often been referred to as the Rwandan Genocide, an unfathomable series of events in 1994 where for about a hundred days, approximately one million total Rwandans were killed, including more than 800,000 minority Tutsis at the hands of extremist Hutus. The reasons are complex. It involves decades of painful history, dehumanization, dangerous policies, and colonization at the hands of Belgium, but what's not complex is that Rwandans killed Rwandans. Family killed family. Neighbors killed neighbors. Even some husbands killed their Tutsi wives. Christians killed fellow Christians. What makes this tragedy even more incredulous is that during the time of the genocide, both ethnic groups were predominantly Christian, "as over 90% of the Rwandan population claimed and still claims adherence to the Christian faith."[2]

As I walked through the halls and exhibits of the Rwandan Genocide Memorial in Kigali (where it's reported that about 250,000 victims were brought to be buried), I could only ask the question, *"How could this happen?"*

As hard as it is to believe (or don't want to believe), many places of worship—churches and parishes of various sizes and denominations—were complicit in the evil of the genocide. Places like Ntarama Church, where more than 5,000 people were massacred by Hutu soldiers and militias. Indeed, many places of worship became "death traps. "[3] During our time there, we had the privilege and burden of hearing from both victims and perpetrators, from citizens and government officials, and from Catholic and Protestant leaders and pastors. They gave us a stern warning about the dangers of placing any allegiance above our obedience to Jesus Christ and the kingdom of God. In essence, the dangers of cultural Christianity.

They obviously wished that this had never taken place in their country's (and church's) history. And yet, they made it clear that they didn't want to be known only by the horrors and evils of the genocide but that truth telling, confession, forgiveness, and reconciliation could be possible. Through pain and tragedy, Rwanda has much to teach the rest of the world. They have much to teach American leaders. They have much to teach American pastors and the church. In a country where some often boast of our Christian roots and identity, the lesson again is that there's a distinct and dangerous difference between cultural Christianity and following Jesus Christ.

We'll tackle these various tensions and temptations, but the heart of this book is to tend to fellow Christians who deeply care about our society, church, culture, and politics … and who want to engage but don't quite know how to navigate this messy and chaotic space. Sound familiar? As a pastor, I've heard this countless times, *"I care. I want to care. I just don't know how to go about it."*

You're not alone. I'm wrestling too. It feels jarring. So many of us are wondering how we can be faithful to Christ, remain engaged, and maintain our integrity. In other words, how can we continue to be Christlike in the chaos and craziness of our political climate?

In this endeavor, there are three realities to be mindful of as you engage this book:

1. This isn't a comprehensive book that covers global politics. It focuses mostly on North American Christians and American politics, and thus, while much of the content can be applied to global Christians, it will require some work of contextualizing what you read into your respective space. While I care about our larger global context, it's not realistic to write a book that covers such an expansive perspective.

2. I love books and I'll utilize many throughout this book, but several of the resources I cite are digital. In many ways, it speaks to both how information is being distributed and consumed and the pace in which events are occurring in our society.

3. And lastly, if this book is remotely pulling its weight, it should challenge and, at times, upset people from various political sides. For someone who wrestles with wanting to be liked by everybody and avoiding conflict, this is absolutely the worst possible book to write. As we all know, there are two topics that shouldn't be discussed: religion

and politics. Oh well. I'm certain that every single person who reads this book will disagree with something, if not many things … and that's okay. While those who are firmly entrenched in their views, camps, and tribes may find little use for this book except to disagree with me, I'm hopeful there are many in between who might be both encouraged and challenged to more faithfully and deeply embody their faith in Jesus Christ.

It's not my intent to tell people who to vote for or how to vote on any specific issues—although, I'll certainly talk about some issues and why it's so critical for us to use prayerful discernment through the lens of Scripture and the life of Christ. The aim is not to be prescriptive on what or who to vote for but rather descriptive in our identity as followers of Christ. Even then, I suspect this book will solicit, as I shared earlier, many criticisms from the Left, the Right, and everyone in between. I've heard many of them already:

"You can't play both sides."
"You're too cowardly."
"You have no backbone."
"You're being too political."
"You're too privileged."
"Why can't you just focus on Jesus?"
"What kind of pastor are you?"

To some, you're too conservative. To others, you're too liberal. To be a Christ follower is to be faithful amid tension. To stay engaged, to remain hopeful, to love anyway, to walk with integrity, and to bear witness to the love, mercy, and grace of Christ. This is becoming increasingly difficult, but such is our call as followers of Jesus. It's not merely what we believe but also *how* we engage.

As you will read in the chapters ahead, I don't believe government in and of itself is a solution for all of society's ills. However, government plays a significant role, and how we engage in the process of governance is of critical importance. My hope is that this book is for all of us, whether we identify as red, blue, purple, or any other color of the political spectrum. You may be obsessed with politics, hanging on every maneuver, every strategic wrangling, completely bought into the game. You may be defending your favored party's positions steadfastly. You may be hopeful, believing that we finally have leaders who get it. You see that God is at work and our prayers have been answered with the leaders in place. Or you may be dismayed but optimistic, believing politics has value and better days are ahead. I am encouraged by the participation we see in politics today, not necessarily because of the political decisions themselves, but because so many Americans are rising to the occasion to vote.

For example, in the 2018 midyear election, almost half of all possible voters actually voted. More than 47 percent of people cast ballots in the 2018 midterms, the highest midterm turnout in more than 50 years.[4]

But maybe you didn't make it to the polls during the last election. You are ambivalent about politics but willing to engage if the right leaders with the right ideas ever come along. That's not an uncommon scenario, and we have different reasons for disengaging. If this describes you, I am sure you have your own unique reasons why. Maybe you've disengaged because you've come to the opinion that politics and government are evil. Diabolical. It's simply not the place for Christians to be. You stay out of it to focus on things that are spiritual and holy, as this world is not our ultimate home.

Maybe you have become cynical and even exhausted. Perhaps you more strongly believed in the political process at some point, but no longer. You may see occasional value in political action and advocacy, but time and again you have seen that our political process is broken beyond repair. So you've decided instead to choose other battles in life and leave political fights for someone else.

I understand. I sometimes feel burned out. Disillusioned. Even deeply discouraged at times because of politics.

But I want to encourage you, believer. Take heart. There is a different way.

Hear this well: *Politics matter.* They matter because politics inform policies that ultimately impact people. When I read the Bible, it's emphatically clear that *people matter to God*—including and especially people who are marginalized, oppressed, forgotten, and on the fringes of our larger society. While some Christians have chosen to disengage from the political process, remain silent, or retreat to the sidelines, that kind of isolation or retreat from society is not endorsed by this book. I believe Christians ought to engage our larger culture—including the many facets and nuances of what we label "politics."

On the other hand, we're living in a cultural context in which it appears and certainly feels as if politics have consumed our lives. Politics not only fill the airwaves of our 24-7 cable news culture but can inundate our daily lives—in conversations, marketplaces, dinner meals, and yes, even within our churches. Now, this isn't necessarily a bad thing, but it *can* become toxic if not rooted in a strong biblical and theological foundation. Why? Because the idolatry of politics is eating away at the civic discourse of our nation. But it's not just in our nation; it's happening within the Christian community as well.

Since politics is a necessary process of any healthy society, this book is exactly that—a practical resource to help Christians navigate the chaotic and turbulent winds of political engagement, not as an end to itself, but as an expression of our discipleship as followers of Jesus Christ. In the chapters ahead, I urge believers not to go to bed with political parties and their powerful politicians. In doing so, we lose the prophetic ability to speak *truth* to power. As I've shared already and will continue to repeat, I'm not suggesting that Christians stand on the sidelines. But we shouldn't ever profess blind loyalty to a party. And by party, I mean *any* party.

This is much of what's happening today. Cultural "Christianity" has bowed to political loyalties. It's neither radical nor countercultural in the way of Jesus. Rather, it's a bastardized and infected form of cultural Christianity. Another word for what I just described is *idolatry*.

Consider the sharp rebuke from Thomas Merton for both progressives and conservatives alike:

> I see little real substance in the noisy agitations of progressives who claim to be renewing the Church and who are either riding some rather silly bandwagon or caught up in factional rivalries. As for conservatives they are utterly depressing in their tenacious clinging to meaningless symbols of dead power. Their baroque inertia, their legalism. Disgust.[5]

Remember, as believers of Jesus Christ, we are to "seek first the kingdom of God" (Matt. 6:33 NKJV) and not the kingdom of our party or respective country. And since this statement likely will elicit strong pushback and feelings, please note there's a big difference between patriotism and nationalism. Go ahead, be patriotic. I am! I am an immigrant and a child of parents who were born in what is now called North Korea. When they were children, there was only one Korea before the devastating Korean War separated and divided both a nation and millions of families. We immigrated in 1977 when I was six years old. I am one of the millions of immigrants who made their way to the United States, and while my story might be unique, I'm a proud, naturalized American citizen who would be quick to share with others the important distinction between patriotism and nationalism.

Nationalism points to a potentially dangerous view of exceptionalism. For example (and for those who identify as Americans), the idea of American exceptionalism can be a dangerous guise for American supremacism. In other words, it functions purely through the lens of worldly power and will do anything to obtain or preserve that power. Now imagine the countercultural stories of Jesus Christ, who must be the central figure of our theology, worship, and life. For example, we must remember the story of Jesus washing the feet of His disciples—especially in a cultural context in which teachers of the law instructed Jewish people not to wash the feet of others because it was considered too menial and dirty. Jesus washing feet is truly radical. This is mind blowing and heart transforming.

We are inundated by politics, party, and power in these confusing times, but this is precisely why we must be about the kingdom of God. If you feel hazy about what the kingdom of God looks like, *look to Jesus*.

He's not a domesticated puppet of our worldly power structures. The crucified and risen Christ is Lord and Savior. Indeed, we must keep looking to Jesus. Better yet, we must make sure we don't just admire Him from afar but actually worship and follow Jesus—His words, His teachings, and His ways.

CHAPTER 1

THOU SHALT NOT GO TO BED WITH POLITICAL PARTIES

It was late on a Tuesday night in November, long past the kids' bedtime, yet I could hear they were still up, playing in their rooms with friends. The adults were packed in our living room, with a bowl of popcorn and mostly devoured party food scattered across the carpet and sofa table. My friends can be slobs.

My wife and I, along with several other couples from church, were leaning into the blue light of the television like mosquitoes to a bug zapper. I glanced around the room at my wife and friends. Some people were standing, some sitting. A few guests were clutching their phones, heads down, refreshing for updates, then scrolling, scrolling, scrolling.

I found worried faces glued to the TV. One friend had her arms crossed, as if to deflect the pain of what political analysts had predicted. Our night had begun with jokes and laughter, but now, hours later, we were silent, with only the commentary of cable news pundits filling the room. The electoral college tally was adding up. We saw the numbers on the bottom of the screen, and what those numbers showed was ominous. We started to imagine what life would be like if, heaven forbid, this man came into power as president.

Then, it happened.

A flashy graphic slid across the screen with a swoosh, accompanied by overly dramatic music. Then the news anchor made the big announcement, affirming as true what the political analysts said might be coming. It was a definitive statement, one that we had worried was remotely possible, but one we didn't dream would actually come to pass.

He had won.

He was becoming president.

The one we had feared.

What would become of our country?

How could this happen to us?

How would we endure life under a person who so clearly did not share our values, our Christian values? How had our prayers not been answered?

In the silence of the room, as we absorbed the weight of this news, it felt as if we were under attack. We were about to enter a dark period, four years of trial for Christians.

We had lost.

(Imagine more dramatic music here.)

NO ONE PARTY IS PERFECT

Does this story sound familiar? Or perhaps, a complete opposite version of the story would. Replace the emotions of fear and incredulity with expressions of elated joy and thoughts of *Our prayers have been answered!*

This story might have real elements for me, but it's a fictional illustration. It's one I've heard before, and an idea I've used in sermons. It exposes something that is true for so many of us.

We pray, advocate, share on social media, and sometimes we hear sermons about Christian values and what they should mean to us in politics. And yet, our world and seemingly our very lives come crashing down when we see someone come to power who we believe is incompatible with our values. What you may have noticed in the illustration above is that I intentionally did not include the identity of the candidate who won, or the respective party.

Many readers of this book likely identify as Christians, but contrary to what you might have heard, Christians are not a homogeneous group that thinks alike on all matters, including the complex, nuanced world of politics. We possess diverse political views, just like non-Christians. Right or wrong, the way we choose to animate our faith in the world is unique to each of us. So when you heard the election night story, you probably imagined a particular politician or party affiliation as the winner of this nightmare scenario.

For some, this outcome could have happened in November 2016.

For others, November 2012.

Or maybe it was November 2008.

Or even November 2004, 2000, 1996, 1992 …

And while I can't predict who, male or female, will win future elections for the presidency, I can guarantee that this story will play out again in 2020, 2024, 2028, and every future election until the day that Jesus returns to restore all things back unto Himself.

Many Christians are not only passionate about politics but are also involved in politics on some level. And yet, I would argue, at times, we are *played* by politics. At times, our identities and values become distorted, and our hopes misplaced.

Elections and politics are often, if not always, advertised as the most important subjects in human history that will forever change the course of the future and determine the fate of our lives, our children's lives, and the lives of our children's children. *(Cue more dramatic music.)*

Every election matters. It's naive to say otherwise, but no political commentator's election night announcement can beat the fact that we already have good news—the ultimate Good News. No candidate or party platform is more important than this. In the heat of a political moment, we tend to forget this truth. Confronted by the realities of unfairness and injustice, pain and atrocities, it's easy to forget. Faced with difficult and overwhelming theological questions, it's easy to forget. This is why we need to keep reminding ourselves the assurance of scriptures from the very lips of Jesus Himself:

> I have told you these things, so that in me you may
> have peace. In this world you will have trouble. But
> take heart! I have overcome the world. (John 16:33)

Many Christians and non-Christians are at times behaving horribly in the ways they engage in our political discourse. If you want proof, you might find it by scrolling through your Facebook feed for five minutes. We accuse, vilify, and expect the worst from people who do not share our political mind-sets. Many of us have become alienated from family and friends because of this toxicity. Where does this come from, except a belief that a certain political ideology is the most important thing in life? Even believing that a certain political ideology is "God's way"? Don't take the bait. No one party is perfect, and no one party monopolizes the kingdom of God.

FAITH IN CHRIST INFORMS MY VOTE

You might be reading this book and start speculating about my personal politics or leanings. I get it. After all, I'm writing a book about politics. As such, you might bluntly ask, "Eugene, are you a Republican or Democrat? Are you conservative or liberal?"

My answer?

Neither. Wait, what are we talking about? On what issue?

How can anyone possibly identify entirely and exclusively with one political affiliation? In essence, isn't this the reality and danger of identity politics? Why have Christians and Evangelical Christianity subscribed to the temptation to even embed our identity with political parties? The beauty and power of the church are discovered not in the Left-versus-Right political spectrum but in the power of the gospel. We find our meaning and power in the person of Jesus Christ.

Rather than asking about one's politics, we should be asking about our understanding, imagination, and embodiment of the beauty and power of the gospel of Jesus Christ. In other words, the crux of our dilemma is that for some Christians, we've allowed our politics to inform our theology rather than our theology and worship of the Christ informing our politics.

Now, as for voting, I have voted both ways. And while the most accurate answer is that I am what political pundits call an independent voter—even while I acknowledge the criticisms that independent votes receive in political discourse—I see good and danger on both sides and issues I strongly disagree with on both sides.

In truth, I have been on a journey ever since I became a Christ follower at eighteen years old and continue to discern because I still prayerfully wrestle with how my faith in Christ informs the way that I seek to live out the two great commandments of loving God and loving neighbor.

BUT REAL CHRISTIANS VOTE REPUBLICAN, RIGHT?

I had accepted Christ as my Lord and Savior the summer before my freshman year of college and joined a college ministry group shortly after I arrived at UC Davis. As I settled into my new world of Christianity-by-choice, I became connected with believers who cared deeply about the Scriptures, prayer, and following God's will and direction for their lives.

I was eighteen, so I could vote by then, and I grew curious about the impact of my newfound faith on many aspects of my life. In conversations with my friends and mentors, I had heard one thing regarding politics: *If you are a Christian, you vote Republican.* That was my understanding; there was no further elaboration expected, and I accepted it … initially.

The first time I voted for a president was in 1992, casting a ballot for George H. W. Bush instead of Bill Clinton. My point isn't to share who I voted for but rather to express my memory of being unsettled about reflexively voting for a party—not only of conviction but also out of perceived Christian duty. As a new Christian, I began to ask questions about this. Honestly, the response I received from my Christian friends can be summed up by these three words: *Don't ask questions.*

There was no room for discernment or discussion; it was just a sense that if you were a good Christian, you voted Republican.

As I look back now, I can see a danger in that thought process, in blind allegiance to one particular party, and in this case, the Republican Party. How could one party be in 100 percent alignment with the values espoused by Christ? How could any party?

Several years ago, I was speaking at a Christian leadership conference being held in Atlanta, Georgia. After the day's events, a group of pastors and leaders converged for a late-night meal and conversation. That's one of the best parts of going to these sorts of events—the candid and honest conversations behind the scenes. When our conversation turned to the topic of politics, a couple of ministry leaders shared with me that growing up in the South, they were ingrained from "the moment we were in our moms' tummies" that they were foremost a Christian, then an American, then a Southerner, and finally a Republican. In that order, and all were important to their identity. One of them even joked that in their family living room, right next to the large painting of blue-eyed, blond Jesus, was a picture of Ronald Reagan.

It's true. *Christians must vote Republican.* That's what I heard in my younger years, but ironically, I've now been hearing the exact opposite, particularly as I've resided in left-leaning, progressive Seattle since 1997. And it concerns me. Not because one can't vote Democrat, but both in the larger context and even in the younger demographic of many churches including my own, I hear a different, yet strikingly familiar, response to how Christians should engage politics: Christians, or at least real, "woke," justice-minded Christians *must* vote Democratic.

Or, more specifically, it goes something like this, *"I'm not judging you, but how could you as a Christian vote Republican?"* (with serious eyeroll).

This may seem so strange for you if you live in America's Bible Belt or in many other parts of the country. Perhaps it's an oddity of living here in Seattle, where only 8 percent of the city voted for Donald Trump in the 2016 election,[1] or perhaps it is because I know that so many younger people, millennials, and those in the emerging Gen Z crowd skew to the left politically.[2] But it's surreal to me that I am now seeing the opposite of what I experienced as a new Christian in my youth—perhaps even with more intensity, judgment, and vitriol.

It's an assumption or expectation in Seattle that if you are a Christian, you must vote Democratic, especially in the Trump era. Please don't misunderstand me. I'm not an apologist for President Trump, but I've been floored at how some left-leaning Christians have absolutely no room to consider why some of their fellow brothers and sisters in Christ, even with much reticence and anguish, would vote Republican. While I disagree much with Trump and have criticized him for many of his policies and bullying tactics, I can't possibly heap a broad stroke of judgment on the 62,984,828 human beings who voted for him.

For some, there is no discussion, and if you think otherwise, you are not only wrong but also racist, sexist, misogynist, homophobic, and transphobic and we can't be friends or be in any kind of relationship. And yes, I've been called all those things for simply suggesting that we ought to grant space for people to vote differently. It's eerie because the term *fundamentalist* is generally used to describe unwavering attachment to irreducible Christian beliefs and is often tied to conservative Christian beliefs, but it's apparent that fundamentalism can infect the ideological extremism on both political spectrums.

CHOOSING A DANGEROUS PATH

I fear that many of us have our favorite politicians and they have their political positions, and by and large, we seem to be comfortable with that arrangement without a ton of other critical thinking. We align with our candidates or our party. As such, sometimes the most passionately held beliefs among Christians may not be informed by our life-transforming faith in Christ, but instead originate from our chosen political party or political ideology. Subsequently, the ideology becomes part of our personal identity.

I am not saying we should not be involved in the political process. We should, and I also believe you can affiliate with a political party. I have numerous friends who have chosen to join campaigns, serve on staff, and even some who have chosen to run for political office at different levels. But I am concerned about blind allegiance, for those who blindly submit to a party's ideology. Many of us affirm it day after day, with the news we consume and with our relationships, which are often with people who think like us and align politically with us.

We can make cacophonous noise in our self-insulated choir, but if everyone is making the same noise, we may be deceived into thinking we're making harmonious music. It's quite telling that in our culture today, an increasing number of Christians are that much more prone to advertise and promote their political leanings and views than actually share their identities as Christians, let alone take intentional steps to actually share their faith with others through evangelism.

An aptly named *New York Times* opinion article, "You're Not Going to Change Your Mind," details research done for the University of London's *Journal of Experimental Psychology*. The study was conducted during the incredibly contentious 2016 US presidential election, about the lengths we will go in our minds to believe what we want to, regardless of the facts.[3]

You may have heard about *confirmation bias*, which is the tendency to embrace information that supports our viewpoints. The antidote to confirmation bias is to intentionally expose ourselves to other viewpoints. Add in a chorus of diverse voices and perspectives and your mind will be opened.

But this study looked a bit further into our human nature regarding politics, delving into something called the *desirability bias*, by looking at the perspectives of people prior to the 2016 election between Hillary Clinton and Donald Trump.

The *New York Times* article explains:

> Though there is a clear difference between what you believe and what you want to believe—a pessimist may expect the worst but hope for the best—when it comes to political beliefs, they are frequently aligned.

Here's how this is playing out. When people received desirable evidence—polls suggesting that their preferred candidate was going to win—they took note and incorporated the information into their subsequent belief about which candidate was most likely to win the election. In contrast, those people who received undesirable evidence *barely changed their belief* about which candidate was most likely to win.

Simply put, we want to think what we want to think. And no matter what someone from the other party says, they can do no right. If Trump cured cancer, I sincerely believe there are many on the left who would not give him praise. This wouldn't be a huge problem because, of course, he would praise himself. (Ha ha, that's a joke. Don't hurt me.) But no doubt this would happen the other way as well. If President Obama cured cancer, some on the right would surely find reasons to criticize him.

Followers of Jesus should not be in bed with any of the political parties. Even if one affiliates with a particular party, may we maintain a posture to collaborate, listen, hold accountable, and engage the political system all while understanding that the political system is not our ultimate hope or answer. In addition, we must never lose the courage or conviction to speak prophetically to a group of people because we are lured by the power associated with politics, a leader, or a political party.

When Christians pledge blind allegiance to a political power and its leaders and cannot objectively evaluate what a politician states or espouses, we travel down a dangerous path. We cease to see the world informed first and foremost by the life and teachings of Christ. Instead, when we allow political allegiances to identify us, we distort the Bible to justify our politics and allegiances.

Put another way: this is *idolatry*.

Let's allow the Scriptures and our convictions about Christ and the kingdom of God to inform how we engage the candidates, the political parties, and the election process.

THE GREATEST COMMANDMENTS

When Jesus came to earth, He was clearly tough to argue with, as He had an otherworldly skill of seeing the hearts of others with clarity.

When Jesus was challenged about His authority, a scribe asked Him what commandment was the greatest.

He responded:

> "Love the Lord your God with all your heart and with all your soul and with all your mind and with all your strength." The second is this: "Love your neighbor as yourself." There is no other commandment greater than these. (Mark 12:30–31)

Earlier in His ministry, Jesus had called His disciples and performed miracles, healing the sick. Word spread, and the crowds found Jesus and began to follow Him, as did His disciples. Jesus went up on a mountainside to teach them a different way to think and live, through the Beatitudes.

There He said:

> Blessed are the poor in spirit,
>> for theirs is the kingdom of heaven.
> Blessed are those who mourn,
>> for they will be comforted.
> Blessed are the meek,
>> for they will inherit the earth.
> Blessed are those who hunger and thirst for
>> righteousness,
>> for they will be filled.
> Blessed are the merciful,
>> for they will be shown mercy.

Blessed are the pure in heart,
for they will see God.
Blessed are the peacemakers,
for they will be called children of God.
Blessed are those who are persecuted because of
righteousness,
for theirs is the kingdom of heaven.

Blessed are you when people insult you, persecute you and falsely say all kinds of evil against you because of me. Rejoice and be glad, because great is your reward in heaven, for in the same way they persecuted the prophets who were before you. (Matt. 5:3–12)

As Christians, the totality of the Scriptures guides us, but these two lessons in particular by Jesus—the greatest commandments and the Beatitudes—help inform how we ought to engage our discipleship as followers of Christ as well as how we engage with others and how we engage with politics. As we study and heed the Scriptures, may we also carefully examine and follow the life, lessons, and example of Christ. This is how we set our moral compass. To love God and to love our neighbors as ourselves. To live in the radical way Jesus taught us to live, as expressed through the Sermon on the Mount.

PROPHETS ARE NEVER POPULAR

In the long story of God, we see many examples of what happens when we become comfortable with a dangerous ideology to justify our views and behavior. I think of the prophet Amos and his biting prophetic word for the upper-class people in the Northern Kingdom of Israel, who were levying heavy taxes on the poor and taking bribes. They were not only rich, but they were the ones in authority as well. Amos wrestled with what he saw. It was a kingdom with peace and prosperity, but the wealthy were lazy, always in search of luxury and pleasure, and unconcerned about the poor.

> You lie on beds adorned with ivory
>> and lounge on your couches.
> You dine on choice lambs
>> and fattened calves.
> You strum away on your harps like David
>> and improvise on musical instruments.
> You drink wine by the bowlful
>> and use the finest lotions,
>> but you do not grieve over the ruin of Joseph.
> Therefore you will be among the first to go into exile;
>> your feasting and lounging will end.
>>> (Amos 6:4–7)

And yet, these were God's chosen people. They were religious people, or in other words, church people. Just like us. They knew the songs, knew the Scriptures, offered sacrifices, but their lives did not reflect the heart of God.

It's poignant to consider how one can be religious and yet be distant from the person and character of Jesus. Another example of such dissonance is the story of Jesus at one of the Pharisees' homes in Luke 5:17–26. When word had spread that Jesus was going to be at this home, teachers of the law from the entire region gathered ... only it wasn't with an open heart to learn and listen but rather to scrutinize and analyze. Imagine this: the Messiah they've awaited is in their midst. Literally, in the center of the room, and they can't believe and receive Him. As a pastor, I've learned that cultural Christians are sometimes the most difficult people to lead to Jesus.

Amos had had enough. Or rather, God had had enough. Through Amos, God told the Israelites that He despised their religious feasts and could not stand their assemblies.

> Away with the noise of your songs!
> I will not listen to the music of your harps.
> But let justice roll on like a river,
> righteousness like a never-failing stream!
> (Amos 5:23–24)

Amos predicted that these people would be the first to go into exile. And about a generation later, the Assyrians conquered Israel, scattering the people. The prophecy came true.

If you are reading this and feel dismayed at those wealthy, abusive people, please be reminded that everybody loves to give prophetic words to other people with different views, but we never seem to receive them. We want to preach to others, but we don't preach to ourselves. We love to flip tables, but not our own. We love to expose the privilege in others while rarely considering our own. I confess, I don't like to hear words of rebuke.

The Israelites became comfortable with a mind-set that was based on their own comfort and desires, and if we're honest, we can easily do the same. We can at least *attempt* to justify anything with Scripture. Additionally, in today's culture, we can always find some authority, leader, author, blogger, or expert who will affirm our views, but how much more valuable is it for us to first ground ourselves in Christ and His ways? We must see the greatest commandments of loving God and loving our neighbors as what directs the trajectory of our lives, informing all of our decisions. Otherwise, we will be at the mercy of building our lives and ideology on something as ever-changing as shifting sand.

Want proof? Here is a glimpse of the examples of shifting politics.

WHAT DO WE STAND FOR?

For as long as there have been politics, political alliances and platforms have been fluid. Even before the turn of the millennium, Donald Trump was exploring a presidential bid. He told NBC News in 1999 about his stance on abortion if he were president: "I hate the concept of abortion," he said, but he was "very pro-choice,"[4] responding to a question about whether he would ban partial-birth abortion. As President Trump, he said, "I will always defend the first right in our Declaration of Independence, the right to life," a right he said extended to "unborn children."[5]

Of course, President Trump is not the first politician to have changed his mind—or to have been publicly awkward about where he stands on an issue. In modern politics, Senator John Kerry was asked about his support for a supplemental military-funding bill in 2003, and was infamously quoted as saying, "I actually did vote for the $87 billion before I voted against it."[6] The nuance was that he voted for a version of the bill that paid for military funding by reversing some of

President Bush's tax cuts, before voting against the bill as proposed, though he voted a year earlier to use military force. Convoluted? A lot of folks didn't easily follow the thought process at the time either.

And if you're forty years old or older, you'll remember President Clinton trying to quell accusations about sexual impropriety, saying unequivocally to a phalanx of TV cameras, "I did not have sexual relations with that woman, Miss Lewinsky."[7] Though it was a firmly delivered statement, it was quickly shown to be a lie, and once the scandal unraveled, he was impeached.

These are just a few sad gems in an ever-growing list of politicians who either are not entirely truthful or at the very least are conflicted about where they stand. To me, it is understandable that personal views can evolve in time, through life experiences and maturity. We have to leave space for politicians (and ourselves) in that evolution. I want to be careful about painting a broad stroke of all politicians, but sometimes politicians simply get caught in a lie and then change their answers to whatever tickles the ears and flutters the hearts of their base supporters.

Individual politicians have their challenges, and entire political parties do too, about matters of enormous significance.

THE DEMOCRATIC SHIFTING TIDE OF POLITICAL IDEOLOGY

Today, it's safe to say that the Democratic Party is home to African Americans by a wide margin, with 90 percent voting for Democratic candidate Hillary Clinton in the 2016 election.[8] But that wasn't always the case. In the 1968 presidential election, the party struggled to come to a consensus for a candidate, as southern Democrats were pulling for

Governor George Wallace, a segregationist, instead of Vice President Hubert Humphrey, who eventually claimed the party nomination but lost to Richard Nixon in the general election.[9]

Another example of the shifting tide of political ideology also comes from the same generation of Democrats. It was during the Vietnam War, one of the most difficult and divisive periods of the United States.

Scholar and writer Michael Nelson has documented the changing political tides through the past few decades. He wrote that beginning with Woodrow Wilson and Franklin Roosevelt, Democrats were comfortable promoting the "animating premise of Democratic liberalism, that the federal government has the ability to solve virtually any problem it chooses to take on, domestic or foreign."[10]

John F. Kennedy's escalation of US involvement in Vietnam was consistent with that philosophy. When Lyndon Johnson succeeded Kennedy after his assassination rocked the country, Kennedy's policies persisted. LBJ, more comfortable with domestic affairs, relied on Kennedy's foreign policy advisers, continued the escalation, and was elected in his own right in 1964.

But by the time the 1968 spring primaries began, Johnson faced growing opposition within the party from Senators Eugene McCarthy and Robert Kennedy and withdrew from the race. After Robert Kennedy was assassinated in June of that year, Vice President Hubert Humphrey sealed the nomination without ever winning a primary.

Nelson wrote that "Humphrey wanted to move his party's platform in a slightly dovish direction to placate Kennedy and McCarthy supporters, but he backed off when Johnson told him that doing so would 'endanger American troops,' that he 'would have their blood on my hands.'"[11]

Consequently, the Democratic platform ended up being more hawkish on Vietnam than the Republicans', which at least called for a "de-Americanization" of the war. Thus, through the party dancing to find the right position, the Dems found themselves out of step, the party against war being more militant. Though Humphrey ultimately pledged to end US bombing of North Vietnam, it was too little too late, and he lost narrowly to Richard Nixon.

CHRISTIAN VALUES AND EVANGELICAL INFLUENCERS

One of the great mysteries of American politics since 2016 has been the support of Donald Trump by evangelicals, particularly the white evangelical community. People, religious and otherwise, attributed their rejection of Hillary Clinton to her support of abortion and LGBTQ issues.

Okay, that sort of gets us through the day after the 2016 election. Barely. But I find it puzzling that some evangelical leaders unequivocally lined up behind Trump.

Do you remember William Bennett's *Book of Virtues*, a treasury of great moral stories? With examples from literature and history, it teaches values like honesty, compassion, and responsibility—and it was a favorite in conservative Christian homes twenty-five years ago.

You might also remember the *Focus on the Family* radio program, so popular in evangelical Christian homes in the '80s and '90s. Over the airwaves and in his books, Dr. James Dobson talked about commitment to your spouse, consistent love and discipline for children, and how to sort through the tough moments of life with God's help and moral grounding.

I'm not suggesting that these are perfect examples of Christian faith, but I'd like to position these works with this question: How could American evangelicals move from being all about morality to now supporting a president who flaunts his own sin in the face of all we've been taught to be right and decent? He is a thrice-married former casino owner who bragged to a TV host that he could kiss women at will because he was a star, adding the infamous line about grabbing a woman inappropriately: "You can do anything."[12] To justify his actions by saying he's not a pastor is dangerous and problematic, because it gives license to any Christian who is not a member of the clergy to do whatever he or she wants without consequence.

How can the evangelical community still strongly endorse the president who has said many disparaging, racially incendiary things about many groups, including Mexican immigrants (many of them families) and proclaimed in his first speech as a candidate: "They're bringing drugs. They're bringing crime. They're rapists. And some, I assume, are good people."[13]

No person has lived a blameless life, me included. No politician has either. But objectively speaking, we should acknowledge that President Trump is night and day different from the kind of moral leader that conservative Christians have always sought.

Michael Gerson, a Wheaton College graduate and former speechwriter for President George W. Bush, bemoaned the trend of evangelicals in politics in a rich and nuanced article for the *Atlantic*. It traces the roots of evangelicalism and its history of political involvement on behalf of the oppressed, particularly as abolitionists, to today.

"It is the story of how an influential and culturally confident religious movement became a marginalized and anxious minority seeking political protection under the wing of a man such as Trump, the least traditionally Christian figure—in temperament, behavior, and evident belief—to assume the presidency in living memory," Gerson wrote.

He continued:

> The moral convictions of many evangelical leaders have become a function of their partisan identification. This is not mere gullibility; it is utter corruption. Blinded by political tribalism and hatred for their political opponents, these leaders can't see how they are undermining the causes to which they once dedicated their lives. Little remains of a distinctly Christian public witness.[14]

This disconnect is nowhere more evident than in the willing, eager, and stunning about-face from Rev. Franklin Graham, son of Billy Graham, and one like it from Dr. James Dobson, who once lambasted President Bill Clinton for his own dalliances with women and the truth. On August 27, 1998, a week after Clinton had more or less confessed his affair with Monica Lewinsky following months of denials, Graham published a column in the *Wall Street Journal* in which he blasted Clinton's morality, his penchant for lying about his morality, and the president's insistence that none of it mattered.

"Much of America seems to have succumbed to the notion that what a person does in private has little bearing on his public actions or job performance, even if he is the President of the United States," Graham wrote.

Graham specifically rejected Clinton's claim that his actions were a private matter between him, his wife and daughter, and God.

> But the God of the Bible says that what one does in private does matter. Mr. Clinton's months-long extramarital sexual behavior in the Oval Office now concerns him and the rest of the world, not just his immediate family. If he will lie to or mislead his wife and daughter, those with whom he is most intimate, what will prevent him from doing the same to the American public? Private conduct does have public consequences.

And Clinton's acknowledgment to that point was not enough for Graham.

> The president did not have an "inappropriate relationship" with Monica Lewinsky—he committed adultery. He didn't "mislead" his wife and us—he lied. Acknowledgment must be coupled with genuine remorse. A repentant spirit that says, "I'm sorry. I was wrong. I won't do it again. I ask for your forgiveness," would go a long way toward personal and national healing.[15]

Frankly, it's hard to argue with that rationale. Clinton's initial reactions to accusations regarding Lewinsky had been defiant. He did, however, offer a far more repentant mea culpa at the September 12,

1998, National Prayer Breakfast, where he told a roomful of clergy, "It is important to me that everybody who has been hurt know that the sorrow I feel is genuine: first, and most important, my family; also my friends, my staff, my Cabinet, Monica Lewinsky and her family, and the American people. I have asked all for their forgiveness."

A cynic, or just an honest recount, would have to add that Clinton's tearful confession came just hours before the release of the painfully detailed report by Special Prosecutor Kenneth Starr, which forever changed our thoughts about cigars and a blue dress from the Gap.

Two decades later, and well into Graham's public support of Trump, even his attitude toward Clinton had magically softened. He told Eliza Griswold, a writer for the *New Yorker*, "Well, you take American Presidents in the past. Bill Clinton wasn't the first man to have an affair in the White House. We're all flawed, and the Bible says we're all sinners. And the Bible tells us that God sent his son to take our sins, to die for our sins."[16]

He's called Trump "a changed person," referred to his affairs as "alleged" even after the payoff to porn star Stormy Daniels by Trump attorney Michael Cohen was established as fact. And Graham accepted from Trump the same tailored acknowledgment he had once rejected in Clinton: "Trump has admitted his faults and has apologized to his wife and his daughter [he didn't clarify which daughter] for things he has done and said. And he has to stand before God for those things."[17]

Dobson's reversal is just as striking. Just days after Graham's 1998 *Wall Street Journal* column appeared, Dobson wrote a letter to his followers in which he went into great detail about Clinton's sexual foibles, his lies, and his visit to Russia as a young man.

How did our beloved nation find itself in this sorry mess? I believe it began not with the Lewinsky affair, but many years earlier. There was plenty of evidence during the first Presidential election that Bill Clinton had a moral problem. His affair with Gennifer Flowers, which he now admits to having lied about, was rationalized by the American people. He lied about dodging the draft, and then concocted an incredulous explanation that changed his story. He visited the Soviet Union and other hostile countries during the Vietnam War, claiming that he was only an "observer."[18]

Yet during the 2016 presidential campaign, Dobson was emphatic—more so than Graham—in his support for Trump, who he famously described as a "baby Christian."

If anything, this man is a baby Christian who doesn't have a clue about how believers think, talk and act. All I can tell you is that we have only two choices, Hillary or Donald. Hillary scares me to death. And, if Christians stay home because he isn't a better candidate, Hillary will run the world for perhaps eight years. The very thought of that haunts my nights and days.[19]

Evangelicals have followed their leaders, and I'm not just talking about leaders like Trump. They follow leaders like Graham and

Dobson, who have guided the faithful to Trump. These two men and other vocal mouthpieces of evangelicalism directly steer Christians toward political conclusions. But let me ask, what would these men have said about Trump twenty or thirty years ago if he were running as a Democrat?

We should be circumspect in all evangelical leaders who dole out political advice. I'll include myself in that statement. I am not perfect, so measure anything in this book with the Scriptures. Let the Word and the life and teachings of Christ be our source of guidance and inspiration.

WE HAVE NO POLITICAL HOME

Our home is not in a political party; our home is in Christ and this new way of living. But does that mean we ignore politics? Clearly no, as politics impact people—and we are called to love our neighbors.

Michael Wear is the author of the book *Reclaiming Hope: Lessons Learned in the Obama White House about the Future of Faith in America*. Wear directed faith outreach for President Obama's 2012 reelection and eventually became one of the youngest White House staffers in modern American history. I actually met Wear through the White House Office of Faith-Based and Neighborhood Partnerships. They hosted the annual Easter prayer breakfast for a group of about 120 Christian faith leaders from very diverse backgrounds. Even as a staffer for the 44th president of the United States, Wear had this important word to say about the danger of finding our home in politics:

Politics is causing great spiritual harm and a big reason for that is people are going to politics to have their inner needs met. Politics does a poor job of meeting inner needs, but politicians will suggest they can do it if it will get them votes. The state of our politics is a reflection of the state of our souls.[20]

Christian historian and author Diana Butler Bass wrote that in AD 410, Rome—a seemingly Christian city—fell to a barbarian invader, getting hit with the worst possible news. Rome was the home of the early church, and Christians there were petrified that this could happen.

"Christians had forgotten that they were citizens of two cities, the one Augustine called 'the City of Man' and 'the City of God.'" They conflated the two into one, fully identifying Roman interests with Jesus' way.

She continued:

Although Rome had accommodated the faith for a time, Augustine believed that Rome was the "City of Man," whose way of life ultimately was founded upon self-love, domination, possessions and glory. Augustine contrasted that way to the Christian way expressed in the "City of God," the pilgrimage community that loves God, seeks wisdom, and practices charity and hospitality. "In truth," Augustine wrote, "these two cities are entangled together in this world. Sometimes the City of Man honors the City of God and its virtues, other times not. For those who follow

Christ, their true home is God's city—always purer
and more beautiful than any earthly one."[21]

To be a faithful Christian is to embrace tension. The mistake some
Christians make is to think we could actually find a home, especially
in politics.[22]

When people have this mind-set, it perpetuates the idea that there
is exclusively one way to engage in politics in order to be a faithful
Christian. And with such a narrow ideology, we can fall into a situation where we stop thinking, stop engaging, and stop asking important
questions.

It becomes my camp versus your camp, in or out, for or against,
friend or foe, ally or enemy. We write off people who identify with the
other party, for whatever reason, and often those reasons are the ones
spread by our chosen media sources.

Jesus died and extended grace for the Left, the Right, and everyone
in between. So, even as we seek to speak truth to power, we must stop
vilifying and demonizing those we disagree with.

It is impossible to have one party that fully encapsulates what it
means to be about the kingdom of God. It doesn't exist. The kingdom of God cannot be encapsulated by one gender, one church, one
denomination, one leader, and certainly not by one political party—
even if there are prominent Christian leaders advocating for it.

WHAT'S ON YOUR HEART AND MIND?

1. How do you respond when someone asks what political party you
subscribe to?

2. How much does your faith guide your political choices? Do you research the issues yourself, or do you rely on Christian leaders to inform you?

3. Think of three political issues that are important to you personally. How much research have you done in order to be fully informed about them?

CHAPTER 2

THOU SHALT NOT BE A JERK

One of the most critical questions Christians must be asking ourselves is, "Are we more in love with the *idea* of following Jesus than actually following Jesus?"

It's a question I wrestle with myself. As a "professional" clergy, I'm amazed at how, in very subtle and seductive ways, I can be tempted to play the game of Christianity rather than take on the radical, passionate pursuit of worshipping and following Jesus.

To be more blunt:

Do we really believe in Jesus?

Do we really believe that Jesus is Lord and Savior?

Do we really believe in the life of Jesus?

Do we really believe that Jesus is still in control, that He is sovereign?

And as such, do we really believe in the words and teachings of Jesus because "sometimes, we can't truly understand the Bible until we obey it"?[1] It's an important question because there are some hard teachings from Jesus. Now, obviously, nowhere in the Gospels do we have any recording of Jesus actually saying, "Don't be a jerk," but He certainly conveys and embodies a life that is antithetical to being a jerk. Jesus exudes tenderness and meekness; His life reflects mercy, justice, and kindness.

Jesus fights for the widows, the marginalized, the poor. Jesus sees the forgotten; He embraces the sick; He welcomes children; He empowers women.

Dr. Russell Moore, president of the Ethics and Religious Liberty Commission of the Southern Baptist Convention, wrote about how Christians should engage culture in our modern era and painted a beautiful picture of the upside-down ways of God.

Moore said if Christians seem to have ceded moral ground in the recent years, they need to speak to the complex social challenges facing us with bigger vision in mind, looking at the world with the lens of the kingdom of God. He called it "the freakishness of the gospel, which is what gives it its power in the first place."

From his book *Onward: Engaging the Culture without Losing the Gospel*:

> The kingdom of God turns the Darwinist narrative of the survival of the fittest upside down (Acts 17:6–7). When the church honors and cares for the vulnerable among us, we are not showing charity. We are simply recognizing the way the world really works, at least in the long run. The child with Down syndrome on

the fifth row from the back in your church, he's not a "ministry project." He's a future king of the universe. The immigrant woman who scrubs toilets every day on hands and knees, and can barely speak enough English to sing along with your praise choruses, she's not a problem to be solved. She's a future queen of the cosmos, a joint-heir with Christ....

The first step to cultural influence is not to contextualize to the present, but to contextualize to the future, and the future is awfully strange, even to us.[2]

Jesus' teachings and actions confounded nearly everyone when He walked the earth—including His own family and His disciples who spent nearly every day with Him during His three years of public ministry—and they still do today. In order to live the kingdom way of living, we must routinely question our mind-sets and, certainly, our hearts too. We must remind ourselves again and again of the way of God, which is usually different from the way of the world. Without remembering what Christ taught us, without constant introspection, we shortchange the power of God's work in and through us.

When Jesus says to turn the other cheek, do we believe His words?

When Jesus says to drop our swords, do we believe His words?

When Jesus says to forgive and love our enemies, do we believe His words?

Over the years, I've experienced difficult and painful actions against me. Some people have fabricated outrageous lies about me because of my faith as a Christian and my influence as a pastor. I have been gossiped about and slandered. Some people have disagreed with my views about immigration and shouted for me to "Go back home." Some have disagreed with my views on gun violence and gun control, and someone even doctored a video to accuse me of being a mass shooter. Someone threw rocks into our church building because they didn't agree with my traditional and historical view of human sexuality. Some have taken personal email correspondences between us and, without permission, published them in their blogs, social media, and newspapers. On two occasions, we've received death threats on me and my family, and during one of those situations, I subsequently had to move my family out of Seattle for some time for fear of their safety.

Such craziness.

And here's another confession: each time, I've wanted to return harm for harm, as in throw bigger rocks, hurl worse insults, fabricate more outrageous lies, shout louder, make bigger signs, and so forth; but this is precisely why we need to remind ourselves who we are, what we're about, and most importantly, who we worship. The *who* makes all the difference. We can't merely be intellectual or cultural Christians who become pawns in a political chess game. As Christians, our integrity still matters. Our commitment to truth telling still matters. Our commitment to justice and the vulnerable still matters. Our commitment to grace and mercy still matters.

Why do these things still matter?

Because our commitment to Jesus *and* His ways still matters.

Church, disagreeing with someone's politics, views, religion, and ideology is never permission to harass or bully that person. And certainly, it's never okay to threaten their well-being. Don't do it. And don't let people you know do it.

In other words, don't be a jerk for Jesus.

THE CONSEQUENCES OF BEING OBSESSED WITH WINNING

Even after tearing both Achilles tendons and blowing out both knees playing basketball over the years, I still can't get enough of the sport. As I tell my kids, Jesus is Lord, but *Ball is Life*. As such, I do love a good game of pickup basketball.

One particular game stands out in my mind. I'm thinking it was probably around 2006, and my 5'8" self was ready to hoop. Okay, 5'8" is being very generous, but with shoes and puffed-up hair, I can hit that height easy. My team at the time was Quest Church, and my position was lead pastor and also self-appointed starting point guard. I entered the gym of Seattle Pacific University, a local Christian college near my home. It was an average night—just a game of pickup basketball with some Questers, their friends, and others—but I must have had a sense of pride on my mind. I was pushing forty, the oldest player on the court, and I was not about to let these twentysomething guys get the best of me.

It was supposed to be a casual pickup, Christian fellowship, get to know one another, outreach, kumbaya kind of basketball outing, but I sometimes let the competitive side of my personality take over. And by sometimes, I mean always. I was trash-talking like Jordan—minus his game and the Air Jordan sneakers. It wasn't just tit for tat; I was escalating things and particularly getting in the face of a random guy who had accompanied his friend from Quest. Now mind you, this was supposed to be a venue to welcome our friends who were interested in learning more about church and, most importantly, about Jesus.

Anyway, after this fateful basketball game, one of the other players, a man in his midtwenties, came up to me and said:

I know who you are. I know you're a pastor. In fact, I have been checking out your church. How you acted on the court today was absolutely embarrassing. Because of you, I don't know if I'd ever come back to not just your church, but any church.

Wow. What a wake-up call. I was embarrassed. I knew what this man had said was true, and I was immediately convicted and profusely apologized. Later, a longtime Quest member who was at the game followed up with me as well. And another. What had gotten into me? I had not acted like a Christian; in fact, I had acted contrary to how Jesus told us to act. It's one thing to be competitive, but I had been so obsessed with winning that I had lacked any semblance of sportsmanship, respect, and civility. As I had played, I had been arrogant and incredibly mean spirited. It was embarrassing and painful to lack such self-awareness.

To put it simply, I was a jerk. With a capital *J*.

I'm not saying that we can't be competitive in life. But when we're more obsessed with winning and being right, when we're more obsessed with power and privilege, more obsessed with winning culture wars, and when we act and speak in ways that are completely antithetical to what we say we believe as followers of Christ, people—fellow Christians and non-Christians—can't help but see the dissonance. And well, it has consequences.

I don't know how many times I have played back that game in my mind, or how many times I have prayed for the young man who said he was unlikely to come back to any church because of my behavior. My point is, when Christians—regardless of our political leanings—behave like jerks and justify our behavior at all costs because of our ideological convictions, we bear false witness to Jesus Christ.

WE DON'T NEED MORE JERKS FOR JESUS

It often feels like Christians get a bad rap. Sometimes we can be characterized unfairly in popular media. It's true that Christians have a PR problem, and too frequently we are defined by what we are against rather than what we are for. Some of us are quite vocal, and that's defining all of us. While the Bible mentions nearly two thousand references to the need to advocate for the poor and pursue justice, we seem to be focused on hot-button social issues as our defining identifier.[3]

Wouldn't it be amazing if the world clearly saw us as embodying the great commandments to love God and love our neighbors? Unfortunately, that's not the first thing that comes to mind for most non-Christians, though. The Barna Group surveyed young non-Christians in America about the top characteristics of Christians, and these are the top three descriptors:[4]

1. Antigay
2. Judgmental
3. Hypocritical

That's unfortunate, to say the least.

As author and activist Shane Claiborne pointed out when he was also dismayed by this research, nowhere in the findings does it mention that Christians are loving, which is how Jesus said we will be known.

Nor are we described by the fruits of the Spirit—you know, the characteristics of God—joy, peace, patience, kindness, goodness, faithfulness, self-control, and love. Claiborne said:

> It's clear that we have become known for some of the very things that Jesus spoke out against, like self-righteousness, and we haven't been known for how we love like Jesus loved. We've become known more for who we've excluded than for who we've embraced, more for what we're against than what we are for.[5]

To be sure, not every Christian is like Fred Phelps, the inflammatory pastor behind Westboro Baptist Church who protests military funerals because of homosexuality in America. (I struggle to understand the logic.) But then again, not every Christian is Mother Teresa. We are pulled between the culture and values we know we should prize, and the societal and human inclinations to judge and categorize. Everything and everyone have their place, and by this logic, if you are not with me, you are against me.

And perhaps in no area of life is this "my way or the highway" mentality clearer than in politics. We'll point to research in a bit, but for a moment, can we simply agree that wading into current political discussions is the equivalent of bathing in a cesspool? Especially in election seasons?

We must learn to be civil with one another, including those we disagree with—even political candidates. This is one of the great challenges in our culture today. We are called to love one another, including those who don't look like us, feel like us, think like us … or vote like us.

In voicing and pursuing our convictions, we not only represent ourselves as followers of Christ; we represent Christ. This is not to suggest we can't have fierce convictions, but there is a distinction between being passionate about our convictions and being mean spirited and jerks. This is worth repeating: Be careful not to dehumanize those you disagree with. In our self-righteousness, we can become the very things we criticize in others.

There is a difference.

I'm all for contending for convictions, but let's not be jerks in the process. Be respectful. Be mature. Be wise. The world doesn't need more *jerks for Jesus.*

SHROUD OF ANONYMITY

Christians are better than average on the jerkiness gauge, right? We're more civil? Please tell me we are! Anyone? Bueller?

By this point, you might be able to predict the answer.

If you want to see the worst in some of your friends or family, or perhaps the worst in yourself, just wade into a challenging issue. Whether you are atheist or faith-filled believer, devoted Christian or Grand Wizard of the Church of the Trees, you know people can be terrible online and in political discussions. And sadly, not much differentiates Christians from nonbelievers—even when Christians interact on many Christian websites.

Dr. Doug Mendenhall of Abilene Christian University measured the incivility of posts and responses across religious and political sites, looking at official blogs that were affiliated with ten major denominations.

He learned that while there was strong potential for disagreement among the denominational sites given the tendency of evangelicals to support Republican candidates and causes while the mainstream denominations favor Democratic candidates and liberal causes, the official sites "consistently demonstrated low incivility in their official blog posts throughout the election year."[6]

So far so good.

Unfortunately, though, unofficial Christian sites closely mirrored the incivility of secular political sites. Mendenhall attributed this to different rules of social behavior between the two groups, even though both were primarily Christian in their perspectives. He also observed that the "shroud of anonymity is much thicker for commenters on the political blogs" than for commenters on either type of Christian site.

Given that research found anonymity for commenters can greatly increase incivility, it was not surprising that on the political sites, where commenters almost never used their own names, incivility was significantly higher than among commenters on either the official or unofficial Christian blogs, where they typically used names or a nicknames that were closely tied to their actual names.

Mendenhall's research also concluded that incivility in the political realm was not the sole property of conservatives or liberals. We are equal-opportunity attackers. But as for those harmed, women in particular are targets of online abuse.

Sarah Sobieraj of Tufts University has published widely on political incivility. Her two-year study concluding in 2018 included in-depth interviews with thirty-eight women who had been the victim of what she terms "digital abuse." She found that aggressors intimidate, shame, and discredit women and regularly "call attention to women's physicality as a way to pull gender—and the male advantage that comes with it—to the fore in digital exchanges."[7]

In an Amnesty International study of tweets sent to female journalists and politicians in the US and the UK, the organization identified 7.1 percent of the tweets as "problematic" or "abusive." The study also found that women of color are particularly victimized by online abuse: 34 percent more likely to receive it than white women. Black women specifically were 84 percent more likely to suffer abuse than white women. And Asian women stood out, as they were 70 percent more likely to receive racist or ethnic slurs than white women.[8] This study did not focus on a Christian population specifically, but this is deeply disturbing nonetheless.

We must stop ignoring this and call it out for the abuse it is. Christians, let's be salt and light in this. And Christian leaders, if we are going to lead with credibility, we also need to show a better way, and when needed, we must be held to account.

WHAT INSPIRES TROLLS?

Why does it always seem to get so bad online, as we dig ourselves into holes from which we can't get out?

Conversations about why interactions on the web and social media have taken such a toxic turn often include speculation about anonymity—the faceless "safety" of the web for trolls and other malcontents. Of course, sometimes we are not anonymous, just absent when we say things online that we would never say in person because our parents and society taught us better.

Some computer scientists from Stanford and Cornell universities examined the problem and identified two factors that influence why people troll.[9] The first is a person's mood. When the experiment was designed to put people in a negative mood, they were much more likely to start trolling. The researchers also discovered that "trolling ebbs and flows with the time of day and day of week." People troll late at night, but infrequently in the morning. And while the researchers didn't speculate about rainy days, Mondays do get people down. Trolling peaks on Monday, ironically enough, the day after church.

The second factor is context. An online conversation that begins with a troll comment is twice as likely to be trolled by others than one that starts without a troll comment. Misery loves company. "The more troll comments in a discussion, the more likely that future participants will also troll the discussion," they said. "Altogether, these results show how the initial comments in a discussion set a strong, lasting precedent for later trolling."

The researchers warn that since trolling is situational, ordinary people can be influenced to troll and spread the behavior to others. "As this negative behavior continues to propagate, trolling can end up becoming the norm in communities if left unchecked."

A psychologist at Stanford has a slightly different take on the problem. In his 2012 research, he concluded that private traits and attributes can be predicted based on responses to social media posts.[10] With about seventy Facebook likes, his program could accurately predict sexual orientation, political affiliation, religious belief, tendencies to substance abuse, and more.

Sociologist Frank Furedi pointed out that believing new technologies will be the end of us is not a new phenomenon. Plato worried that reading and writing would weaken the mind and destroy people's memory. Furedi espoused that the evil on the internet is just the latest iteration of past evils (for example, Neo-Nazis are inspired by racists from the past).[11]

Nevertheless, people are less and less optimistic about the social impact of the internet. A 2018 Pew Research Center study found that the percentage of adults 65 and older who believe that the internet has been mostly good for society has declined 14 points since 2014, from 78 percent to 64 percent. Keep in mind that older adults have been particularly rapid adopters of social media. Younger adults have been more consistent, but even their support has declined, from 79 percent in 2014 to 74 percent in 2018.[12]

RESIST THE TEMPTATION

I am not alone in the temptation to behave like a jerk.

Though we live in an amazing era, with electric cars, K-pop on demand, and unlimited information at our very fingertips via smartphones and other technological devices, our connected world provides such an amazing platform for being a jerk.

Before the advent of the internet, jerks usually needed to be big, physically intimidating bullies, or people who weren't hugged enough as a child, or people in power who never got the memo about kindness. But today, because of the internet and social media, anyone can be a jerk. Even misguided grandmas and pastors can be jerks. We just sit there fuming, spewing our opinions, relevant or not. We say things that almost no one in real life would ever say to another person, and somehow, we're okay with it.

I know I've been a jerk before, but many times it's those close calls of jerkiness that come to mind. I imagine posting something anonymously. And occasionally, I have written something, a nugget to lob into a conversation, but thankfully in most of these circumstances, I decide to delete it before I post.

And sometimes, I'm not that wise.

RELATIONSHIPS ARE KEY

Do your homework. Learn about people. Have a conversation. Start with someone near you … and you might want to consider someone who does not look like you. These interracial relationships make a huge difference in changing perspectives. Even though five decades have passed since the Civil Rights Movement, America remains largely segregated.

A study of social networks among Americans shows this with great clarity. To be clear, the social networks I'm talking about in this study are not social media networks, like Facebook, but the small network of people whom you might discuss important matters with, including close friends or family.

The result of the study: For 75 percent of white people, their close social network was entirely white, with no minority presence. For black people, 65 percent of people said their social networks were all black. Just under half of Hispanics have a core social network that is all Hispanic.[13] To break it down even further:

> In a 100-friend scenario, the average white person
> has 91 white friends; one each of black, Latino,

Asian, mixed race, and other races; and three friends of unknown race. The average black person, on the other hand, has 83 black friends, eight white friends, two Latino friends, zero Asian friends, three mixed race friends, one other race friend and four friends of unknown race.[14]

And we wonder why we often don't understand one another. The point is, we're attempting to have conversations in America about critical issues, but so many of us have no friendships or relationships with people of other races—and probably even fewer conversations with people of other faiths or with people who don't share our viewpoints.

DEHUMANIZATION VERSUS IMAGO DEI

Jesus told the disciples in John 4:4 that "now he had to go through Samaria." I suspect that the disciples were all very concerned about Jesus after this suggestion because, simply, well-knowing Jewish people did not travel through Samaria.

Why?

Starting from a conflict in 2 Kings 7, Samaritans began to be dehumanized or, in other words, thought of as "less than." They were perceived as dirty, unclean, inferior, half-breeds, contaminated, and as a result, vilified and otherized (sadly, seen as "the other"). This only led to deep-seated animosity. Now, multiply that misunderstanding and animosity over generations upon generations. This is why there was such ill will between Jews and Samaritans, which explains why Jesus declared His intent to walk through Samaria.

On this journey, Jesus encountered a Samaritan woman at a well, and with His commitment to both grace and truth, He engaged this woman with such humanity and dignity. The opposite of humanity and dignity is dehumanization and otherizing. When we dehumanize others, it can lead people to the justification of words, actions, and even policies that demean and degrade other people. For example, Nazis referred to Jews as rats, Hutus called Tutsis cockroaches in the Rwandan Genocide, African Americans in the United States—both during slavery and Jim Crow—were compared with apes or monkeys, and in current times, radical monks in Burma refer to the Rohingya minority group as animals.

Of course, this stands in deep contrast to the theology of the Imago Dei (the Image of God). As Christians, we believe that every single human being bears the image of God. We believe that every human being is fearfully and wonderfully made.[15] Don't miss it: Jesus was declaring His politics here. In the kingdom of God, Jesus went through Samaria with a determined and resolute mind to break down barriers of hatred and cultural, ethnic, and racial prejudice to replace them by building bridges of forgiveness, reconciliation, peace, love, and hope.

Jesus was no pushover, and indeed He was quick to stand up and speak out in key moments, like cleansing the temple of merchants and money changers. But how many other times did Jesus exhibit restraint and love to those who did not deserve it? Jesus healed people, forgave them of their sins, and told them to stop sinning. Jesus loved all, time and again, in story after story. It must have been exhausting. At many key moments, Jesus also withdrew to pray—to once again become aligned or "one" with the Father. With that in mind, should we not also pause and ask the Spirit to inform us, to guide our thoughts and actions? That's tough to do when it's so easy to lob a quick and cutting comeback—but a spirit of peace must override our inclination for fire and fury.

To devalue the life of another, to be a jerk, is counter to the kingdom. To be a jerk, to revel in earthly shouting matches, sells short the radically different way of Christ. It's a poor representation of Christianity and also a foolish political move. Before all of our best arguments, let's first show love. That's what we're supposed to be known for, after all.

WHAT'S ON YOUR HEART AND MIND?

1. When you find yourself disagreeing with someone's politics, views, religion, or ideology, what is your usual response? Does it align with kingdom values?

2. In what instances are you quick to stand up and voice your opinion? Whom do you share your opinions with?

3. Have you encountered a "jerk for Jesus"? How influential did that person seem to be?

CHAPTER 3

THOU SHALT LISTEN AND BUILD BRIDGES

The countercultural way of God was spoken through James chapter 1 in the New Testament, when he said believers in humble circumstances should take pride in their high position and the wealthy would fade away like a wildflower. That's certainly not the way of the world, nor is the desire to actually listen, a virtue James extolled immediately afterward:

> My dear brothers and sisters, take note of this: Everyone should be quick to listen, slow to speak and slow to become angry, because human anger does not produce the righteousness that God desires. (James 1:19–20)

We feed on anger and outrage today. It's a sad reality, but our society runs on the currency of fear. And we are too often so slow to listen. I think my wife tells me this, though I cannot be sure.

One of the most profound privileges and responsibilities as a pastor is to welcome people to the Communion table, which declares that the life, death, and resurrection of Jesus are indeed good news for the whole world and that salvation is offered by the grace of Christ to all those who place their trust in Him. Because of the grace and love of Jesus Christ, the church can truly be countercultural in that it welcomes all who profess faith in Jesus Christ to the table.

I can't imagine any other institution that can gather people from all backgrounds, ethnicities, and stories—and even political inclinations or affiliations. When we serve Communion in our churches, we do not have a wine line for the Left, a grape-juice line for the Right, and a gluten-free line for the centrists. I'm reminded of the truly good news declared in Paul's letter to the church in Galatia, which still has deep truth to us today:

> There is neither Jew nor Greek, there is neither slave
> nor free, there is neither male nor female; for you are
> all one in Christ Jesus. (Gal. 3:28 NKJV)

And perhaps we can make this contextual adjustment for our polarizing times:

> There is neither Jew nor Greek, there is neither slave
> nor free, there is neither male nor female, Republican
> nor Democrat; for you are all one in Christ Jesus.

Therefore, we must work to remain in friendship and fellowship. As Christians, we need to agree that the most significant aspects of our relationship are not our politics, our political views, or our political affiliations but that we are connected together as brothers and sisters in Christ.

> Make every effort to keep the unity of the Spirit through the bond of peace. There is one body and one Spirit, just as you were called to one hope when you were called; one Lord, one faith, one baptism; one God and Father of all, who is over all and through all and in all. (Eph. 4:3–6)

Politics has its role. But Christ is the most significant aspect of our community.

DINNER WITH AN ENTRÉE OF EMPATHY

Ah, the holidays. You feel the nip in the air on late fall walks through the neighborhood and smell smoke drifting from fireplaces for the first time of the season.

The weather cools and days shorten, which means that Seattleites mostly go into hibernation mode. You put your hands in your pockets, knowing that Thanksgiving and Christmas are right around the corner. It's time for your annual intake of stuffing and pumpkin pie.

Beyond food, the holidays represent something much more meaningful: reconnecting with family—close and distant. Being together. But it's not all warm and fuzzy. Increasingly, so many of us dread the side dish of the holiday meal: uncomfortable political conversations with extended family at the dinner table.

Raise your hand if that's you!

Maybe you lean politically left and you're worried about Uncle Bud and if he might share some tone-deaf, borderline-racist rambling about immigration and "*those* people." Or perhaps you lean politically right and you're worried about your outspoken socialist nephew, David, and his vegan girlfriend, Ann—who thoroughly confused you because she identified herself as she/her/hers the first time you met her at the same holiday gathering last year.

Holidays have always been a stressful time. But don't these meals seem even more unpleasant because of political discord? No amount of smiling while saying "Pass the potatoes" can change the fact that your aunt is giving you the serious stink eye.

And we know the holiday family gatherings are coming soon because of the inevitable rants on social media. You know how it goes. Jim is upset about having to see Uncle Bud, David, Ann, or Stink-Eye Aunt. What's interesting is that folks who post such stuff don't ever consider that other family members are likely saying or feeling the exact same things about *them*. Self-awareness, anyone?

Turkey and stuffing aside, why would you want to re-create all the uncomfortable parts of a politicized family holiday meal … and have those conversations with strangers?

Incredibly, having dinner with strangers and talking about politics is exactly what came to the mind of an Asian American woman named Justine Lee one day after the 2016 election, the election in which Hillary Clinton called half of Trump's supporters "a basket of deplorables."[1] Yes, this was the same election where Trump invented a mocking nickname for nearly every political enemy and speculated that "Lyin'" Senator Ted Cruz's father might have been in on the assassination of JFK.[2] Yes, the state of politics and the lack of civility seem to be worsening day by day.

The day after the election, Lee had an epiphany. What about gathering people from a variety of political and social backgrounds to talk and share dinner together? Lee was not a political operative; she was a marketer in the San Francisco Bay Area. But she cared about decency, and cared about America, so she and her friend Tria Chang cofounded a group called Make America Dinner Again (MADA).

The group says while people have many venues to protest, donate, and fight, MADA is an avenue to *listen*. The dinners are small, six to ten guests with a variety of political viewpoints. During the evening, facilitators help ensure respectful conversations and guide activities, while everyone shares some good food.

"We think of food and a warm meal as sort of a nice conduit to conversation and understanding," Lee said.[3]

The commonality with all who attend a dinner? They want to know and understand their neighbors in real life who may think or live differently. MADA is about gaining empathy, where perspectives are respectfully aired and unlikely relationships form.

Since the first MADA gathering in San Francisco, the group has grown substantially, with facilitated dinners happening in more than dozens of cities across the country, and now inspiring a UK member of Parliament to host a dinner between people aligning with the "Leave" and "Stay" factions of Brexit.[4]

Among those who have bought into this idea is … wait for it … conservative talk-show host Glenn Beck, who put together his own event for his news outlet, the Blaze, cohosting with a successful gay Hollywood producer named Riaz Patel, who is now friends with Beck.[5]

I was stunned when I heard Beck was on board with this. I've never been a huge Glenn Beck fan, as he's been incredibly divisive. He's said some outrageous things to discourage Christians from pursuing justice, including the recommendation to "run as fast as you can" if you see the phrase "social justice" on your respective church website.[6]

So, when I heard Beck was opening himself up to hear other perspectives, I was skeptical, but also hopeful. Beck said when we talk to folks who aren't like us in a setting like this, our perceived adversary becomes just another person at dinner, regardless if they're on the other end of the political spectrum.

"No matter how much we disagree with the person sitting right next to us, and we were sitting on opposite ends, the most important thing is that we never lost sight of our humanity," Beck said.

The topics for the event hosted by Beck and Patel were not easy. Socialism. Gun laws—and how to reduce shootings. Freedom of speech. Censorship. All important, real, and very messy conversations.

I figured if Glenn Beck checked out MADA, I needed to experience it for myself. So I signed up for the local Seattle chapter of MADA and received a confirmation email after a couple of weeks. Admittedly, I was nervous. I didn't quite know what to expect. Who would be the other guests? Would there be a balance? Would enough conservatives attend? Actually, do any exist in Seattle? Would it begin with respectful listening and eventually disintegrate into shouting, finger-pointing, and MMA fighting? Should I be working out? What would people think of me being a Christian and a pastor ordained in a denomination containing one of the most horrendous words known to progressive Seattleites: *evangelical*? And most importantly, since it's a potluck, what do I bring?

Friday night came along, and a group of seven strangers (including our MADA host) gathered for dinner in the basement of a local church. Go figure. To my surprise, we were an eclectic, multiethnic, and multigenerational group of people: a teacher, a bartender, a pastor, a techie, a college student, a receptionist, and a nonprofit worker. After what was honestly a delicious meal (shout-out to the person who brought those killer chicken wings), we shared our respective stories and what drew us to the gathering. It was clear that while we were all over the map politically, it was our frustration over the political landscape that was the common bond. We discussed abortion, gun control, racism, privilege, immigration, and more. We discussed, shared, listened, discussed, and listened some more. If I'm honest, I cringed a couple of times—especially when someone mentioned we should do away altogether with borders and simply have one human nation.

But that night, what stood out the most for me was meeting Amanda (not her real name). I'm guessing she was probably in her midfifties because she told the group she and her husband were empty nesters. She said she was Republican, voted for Trump, owned some guns, including the one she revealed she was carrying with her, and served at her local church. Additionally, she had been a devoted teacher in a Seattle public school for the past couple of decades. She shared of her pain and experience in Seattle as a Christian—stories similar to those I've heard from other evangelical Christians in our area: mocked, ridiculed, dismissed, ignored, and even bullied.

As a teacher, she pushed back against the decision by the Seattle School District teachers' union to have teachers wear "Black Lives Matter" T-shirts. She made it clear that she wasn't against teachers wearing the BLM shirts but rather every teacher being required to wear them. She emotionally pleaded that she loved her students, including her black and brown students, which was why she kept showing up to work every single day for over twenty years. But she couldn't support the organization because she didn't agree with everything they stood for.

With her head lowered and finding it difficult to make eye contact with the group, Amanda recalled the past couple of years being the most difficult time for her as a teacher because of the subsequent blackballing, ostracizing, and dismissing that took place. Fellow teachers who were once friendly and chatty with her altogether ignored her, especially when rumors circulated that she was ... a Jesus-believing Christian.

After several hours together, our eclectic group of seven didn't solve the ailments of our society and culture. We didn't cancel the national debt. We didn't solve homelessness in our city. We didn't resolve the opioid crisis. We didn't present a proposal for comprehensive immigration reform. We didn't figure out how to construct a gun-control policy. Nope, we didn't fix anything, but we acknowledged that while our views were different, we weren't enemies. We took time to listen, to empathize, and in doing so, we became a little more understanding, a little more human.

And that's my point. It's way too simplistic to reduce others and their views. While it's important for us to acknowledge our views and convictions and, when needed, to speak up and contend for them, it's nearly impossible to have meaningful dialogue, and thus progress, if we have no idea how others feel and why they have those feelings. Civility is impossible without a genuine commitment to listen.

YEARNING TO LISTEN

In December of 2015, then-candidate Donald Trump proposed banning Muslims from entering the United States, restricting an entire religion of people—barring anyone from that religious group who was not already living in America. Trump was speaking at a campaign rally in South Carolina days after a shooting that was believed to have been inspired by the Islamic State terrorist group.

"Donald J. Trump is calling for a total and complete shutdown of Muslims entering the United States until our country's representatives can figure out what the hell is going on," the future president said to cheers at a rally in Mount Pleasant, South Carolina.[7]

The state of South Carolina, meanwhile, is home to few Muslims, a fraction of 1 percent of the population. And nationwide, Muslims remain a small part of the population—just 1.1 percent.[8]

Across the country, in my hometown of Seattle, radio producer Ross Reynolds heard the proposal to ban all Muslims from entry and wondered, *How many non-Muslim Americans even know a Muslim?*

With that question in mind, a new series was born on the local NPR radio station, KUOW. It's called "Ask A ..." and has a similar concept to Make America Dinner Again, an effort to create a transparent and respectful community dialogue about meaty issues.

From KUOW:

> The concept is simple: Get eight people from a group that's in the news and set up conversations with eight people who want to know more about the group. They each have one-to-one conversations until all

have met. Then we have a group discussion and continue the conversations over a meal.

It's a way to break out of our echo chambers and make connections with others in our community.[9]

The first "Ask A ..." segment was "Ask A Muslim," and that topic was repeated two more times. Other segments have also aired, covering topics as diverse as gun control and sexual identity. An early episode was "Ask A Trump Supporter." While it's likely that few people at the Trump rally in South Carolina knew any Muslims, it's also quite likely that not very many people listening to the NPR station in Seattle were tight with Trump supporters.

The folks who agreed to be interviewed in the "Ask A Trump Supporter" event had a variety of perspectives about the president. One woman said she was most pleased about Trump's Supreme Court nominees and most disappointed by Trump's move toward repealing and replacing Obamacare, as the Republicans didn't have a good plan.

Other perspectives from Trump supporters:

"I think he's crazy like a fox."

"He screws up and he just keeps going. He doesn't quit."

"I guess I should have expected that he wouldn't really be ready for some of the details of the work."

The small audience at the radio station studio took in the dialogue, sharing a meal with their new acquaintances, curious about their personal stories and what motivated their perspectives and why.

KUOW says the dinners are so successful, people typically don't want to leave when the events wrap up. Researchers with the station were curious about the impact of these dinners—if they served a purpose beyond being a compelling radio story. Initial findings were promising. KUOW conducted three surveys: before the event, immediately after, and three months after.

Once the people who were asking questions got to know about someone, such as a Trump supporter or a Muslim, they were quizzed about their view of empathy and understanding of the people they interviewed. The findings showed positive feelings toward the group increased after the meetings and stayed higher than pre-event levels long term.

Make Dinner Great Again and Ask A … are both challenging people like you and me to rethink our perspectives, but for many of us, our propensity is still to protect our views, our tribe, or our narrative, however we define it. Getting to know our neighbors is not a onetime vaccination against intolerance. We must stay in relationship with people who are not like us, long term.

LEARNING TO LISTEN IN NEBRASKA

Living in Seattle has given me great visibility to a movement of God in a city that largely seems to be cynical, and at times adversarial, about all things involving religion—especially if it smells anything remotely close to evangelicalism. Seattle is a place of life, innovation, secularism, deep faith, skepticism, and joy. And the stereotypes are largely true. Seattle is quite liberal politically.

As we challenge ourselves to go deep, to be circumspect, to know the issues, it's also of critical importance to get our noses out of books and media and actually engage with others who don't look or think like us. We must expose ourselves to other people and get vulnerable.

One of my biggest revelations and perspective changes has been taking place fifteen hundred miles from here, as I was thinking about fishing—but catching so much insight along the way.

While some people at my church affiliate as Republicans, and over the years I've had numerous conversations and meals with friends and neighbors who lean right, I don't know many Trump supporters personally, so my trips to Nebraska have been enlightening—and humbling. For the past decade, I've taken an annual trip to Nebraska for an extended rest. A week or two of disconnecting from social media, diving into those books that have stacked up on my desk, and lots of solitude for prayer and Scriptures. And I'm an avid fisherman. I also go to Nebraska to hone my skills to pursue my secret ambition to become a professional bass fisherman someday. I'm sort of joking but not. Please sponsor me!

I've been to Nebraska so often that I have met people and developed friendships there. We text. We get together. We have meals. After building relationship and trust, we're able to ask questions and learn about one another's lives, families, hopes, and concerns. I hear their fear and their pain, of not being heard, of feeling forgotten as coastal cities seem to receive most of the attention. I hear from farmers who feel invisible, as their suffering and sacrifice are not highlighted by the press. I remember learning from them about the devastating drought in 2012 and how it impacted nearly every single person in the region. They said it was one of the worst droughts they had experienced since the 1930s.

As I listened to these stories, I realized I hadn't heard a single word about this drought even though I carefully follow the news. I was silent when they asked, "Where was America? Where were you?"

I had an epiphany as I listened to them. It was a moment of déjà vu. Elements of their stories were similar to so many stories I'd heard before, but from people of other races, people aligned with another political party.

If anyone was listening to our conversation and hearing stories about how my Nebraskan friends felt invisible, abandoned, and forgotten, they could walk away thinking they had just heard from someone on the left who felt invisible, abandoned, or forgotten. I know that it sounds corny (get it?), but it reminded me that people have way more in common than we realize.

I was somewhat surprised. In a rural, nearly all-white area, I was recognizing echoes from urban communities. Perhaps a person of color in a majority-white area who feels like all eyes are on them, except when it comes to friendship. Perhaps a refugee who received a lot of love when arriving to this country, but no notable support or community a few months in. Perhaps a single mom who is doing everything she can to make ends meet, but it's never enough.

I heard those same sentiments from hardworking farmers. Feeling as if their opinions were disregarded. Not seeing themselves represented in society. No empathy from the country and its elected leaders for the challenges they were facing. Unemployment or underemployment. Extremely high healthcare costs. Living from paycheck to paycheck with no hope in sight to get ahead and have financial security.

I also asked them, "Have you ever had conversations with people who have voted differently than you?"

It's a question I often ask people in Seattle. All of us need to consider it. Are we intentionally surrounding ourselves with people who have opinions that are not like ours? Do we care enough about our neighbors to get to know them, their backgrounds, their beliefs, their opinions? Do we care enough to go deep in our knowledge about issues that matter to us?

We are shouting about and arguing with groups of people, but we don't have relationships with people in those groups. This can happen to churches also as we develop echo chambers.

I wouldn't have said this the first couple of years I went there, but I look forward to going to Nebraska, not just because of the fishing, but because of the people I would have never met and, thus, understood. It is surprising, but I have seen this come true in my own life. It is possible to befriend people whom you might disagree with on certain issues. It is possible to love and listen to your neighbors, even if they believe something different politically.

We keep learning again and again from the Scriptures, and especially the ministry of Jesus, that relationships matter. And relationships aren't possible if we're unwilling to listen to one another and share our respective stories.

LEARN TO UNDERSTAND

Focus on the Family has become a different organization under the leadership of Jim Daly, since he took the helm after Dr. Dobson. I've enjoyed meeting him on numerous occasions, for meetings at their headquarters in Colorado Springs and even at numerous advocacy gatherings in Washington, DC. One time I had the opportunity to record an interview with him on his radio show in which we discussed many things, including the story of One Day's Wages, a nonprofit that my wife and I began to engage the complex issues of extreme global poverty. Focus on the Family still leans to the right politically but has become a little less political in its identity over the past few years.

I deeply appreciate Daly's desire to be a brave yet humble voice for Christ in the world, but perhaps more than being a voice, I applaud the work he has done to have a listening ear, which is often the bravest action a person can take. In our culture, speaking up has often been praised as courageous. There's certainly some truth to that, but maybe quieting down and listening to others is courageous too. We could all listen more, especially to those who've been silenced historically.

Daly contributed an essay to the book *Still Evangelical?*, outlining his thoughts about the needed posture of Christians as we attempt to engage culture. He wrote:

> As evangelicals engage the world (for that is our full orientation—taking the good news of the gospel of Christ to those outside the church and into the public square), we must remember that no group is monolithic. Just as we don't care for it when people view all Christians as a caricature, we should understand that "the world" isn't monolithic either. Not all atheists are angry with the church and want to steal away our children. Not all college professors and media professionals are "humanists," out to attack Christianity at every turn. Not everyone outside our community hates Christians or dislikes our engagement in the culture. Not even most.[10]

Daly said that because each person is an individual created by God, they're as unique as a snowflake—and we should embrace people in their uniqueness. He continued, saying that Christians should always have two questions in mind as we engage with those around us:

1. Help me understand what you believe.
2. What brought you to those conclusions?

This requires being good listeners. People who met Pope John Paul II throughout his life remarked about what an intense listener he was. It seemed that nothing else existed to him when he engaged with someone. Have you ever spoken with someone like that? If you have, I'm sure you can picture them right now and recall how they made you feel.

In any conversation, political or otherwise, each of us can choose to give the gift of listening to others. That's good news for the future of our world.

BETTER ANGELS FOR AMERICA

Shortly after the 2016 presidential election, three marriage and family therapists with deep experience in helping people talk to each other decided the country needed them. What began as a day of guided conversations between ten Trump supporters and eleven Clinton supporters in South Lebanon, Ohio, grew to become Better Angels, a nonprofit with the declared goal to depolarize America.

In that first day's effort, people discovered they really liked each other. They had things in common. And they didn't have to agree, or change their minds about what they believed, in order to treat each other with respect and kindness. Today, Better Angels plans twenty or more events per month nationwide, some with as few as a dozen participants. They've received national news coverage for this rare idea that people who disagree can talk to one another. Pleasantly.

Every aspect of the organization—its board, staff, event participants—represents red and blue. Keynote speakers at the 2019 national convention included Hawk Newsome, chairman of Black Lives Matter NY, and Alexandra Hudson, educational consultant at the Liberty Fund and a former Trump appointee.

The Better Angels pledge is focused on three simple ideas that many find unlikely to impossible:

- As individuals, we try to understand the other side's point of view, even if we don't agree with it.
- In our communities, we engage those we disagree with, looking for common ground and ways to work together.
- In politics, we support principles that bring us together rather than divide us.[11]

What a concept. Actually getting to know our neighbors rather than vilifying them. It reminds me of something Jesus would do.

BREAKING BREAD—AN INSPIRED IDEA

As I reflect on the many stories of Jesus, it's clear that He loved to eat. So simple. So human. So divine. His first miracle was at a wedding feast, when He changed water into wine. He sought out Levi, a tax collector and thus an enemy of the people, and yet the next thing you know, Jesus is eating with Levi and a group of tax collectors. Jesus taught us a story about love for our neighbors while asking a Samaritan woman for water—all while walking through Samaria, a path few Jews took during those times because of the hostility and tension between them and Samaritans. Also, eating with Mary and Martha and seeing the better way. Feeding the five thousand and so many other stories.

Jesus not only loved to eat; He also loved the connection and community that happens when people sit together and are nourished together. If you want to think of a guy who does not discriminate with his dinner guests, Jesus is example number one.

In Luke 14, Jesus accepted a dinner invitation to the home of a Pharisee. Over this meal, they had tough but real conversations—not online or in cryptic text messages—but over a meal. In person. Face to face.

I think back to the Last Supper and how Jesus willingly ate with Judas. Yes, the same Judas who ate right before he went out to turn Jesus in to the authorities. Jesus shared dinner with the man who would betray and help lead Him to His own execution. It's true, just when we think we get what it means to follow Him, Jesus washes the feet of His disciples, including the man He knew would betray Him, the one who would deny Him, and the others who would abandon Him.

In fact, in the momentous moment that rocked human history, those closest to Jesus still didn't grasp … Jesus. At the same dinner, His disciples jockeyed for positions of power and influence. Who was greater? Who was second in power? Who was next in line? Who would be the right-hand man?

During that meal, Peter pledged to be by Jesus' side always, and yet we know what happened. Peter, the rock, would disown Jesus three times, just a few hours later. Yet Jesus sat down and ate with His family of friends and believers. It was a radical move. It was a move of an all-powerful God who exemplified the way to live.

This love-your-neighbor-kingdom imagination and living is more scandalous and countercultural than we can ever possibly understand—but try we must. This is what it means to not just know about Jesus but to follow Jesus.

Make America Dinner Again and Ask A ... are occasions that bring out the mind-set of Christ in secular situations. But for some of the participants in these events, it's deeply spiritual, as these are the kinds of purposeful encounters that can lead even the jaded among us into God's reconciling work.

The Seattle Chapter head of Make America Dinner Again is a twentysomething woman named Emily Nelson Lewis. She happens to attend my church, Quest, and is married to our student ministry director, Phil Lewis. She is a devoted student of the Scriptures, attending seminary and currently working at the intersection of the arts and church. Emily calls herself a "hospitality artist," which is accurate, considering the finesse needed to bring constructive dialogue and bridge building to something as contentious as politics in our modern era, especially in a polarizing place like Seattle.

The dynamics of race are also real in her own life, as she's Caucasian and married to an African American man. Emily grew up in a small town in Montana with overwhelmingly conservative politics, and Phil was raised in the suburbs of Seattle. Emily says she's been drawn to the idea of MADA because of polarization and brokenness in her own life story—and sees that MADA has given her a chance to point people to the value in each of our stories. Since April of 2018, she and other MADA facilitators have hosted dozens of events, with more than five hundred people sharing dinners together so far.

In describing the MADA dinners, Emily also brings clarity on a related topic. She says her fellow millennials seems to be entirely comfortable cutting others out when relationships become uncomfortable. She calls it "cancel culture," a term that's becoming more common, and it's not describing paring down online subscriptions.

Have you ever been ghosted? Blocked? Unfriended? Emily's words:

> It is easier to unfollow, unsubscribe and delete the existence of those who think, act, vote or live differently than you. When we exclusively engage difficulty online, it becomes easier and more tempting to forget the humanity of others. This is our reality, and it's one that has created a relational gap so wide that we've become paralyzed by the thought of engaging difficult conversations, even with those we'd call friends.

By the nature of a person "canceling" another person, we see how transactional life can be, when life truly is meant to be lived with and for others. Of course, each generation has traits that seem similar, decade after decade, such as young people being categorized as lazy or selfish.

But now, with our ability to make social tribes, we curate people who are just like us, and shut others out. We're comfortable with it. And it's not just a millennial or Gen Y thing. It's something that can influence all of us. Not only is this happening more, but it's being encouraged more. It's not just on the fringes but supported by our political leaders and, sadly, even our church and spiritual leaders. I've heard it preached about and spoken on more occasions than I wish to remember in which church leaders suggest it's good to engage in "cancel culture" for the sake of personal convictions and healthy boundaries. Convictions and healthy boundaries are certainly important, but we need a deeper imagination that goes beyond tribalism and cancel culture.

Through dinners with hundreds of people with a variety of backgrounds, men and women who have each experienced life differently, Emily says she can more easily see the Imago Dei in the people around her. And isn't this the essence of what Jesus taught and embodied throughout His life, death, and resurrection? Church, let's be careful not to dehumanize those we disagree with. In our self-righteousness, we can become the very things we criticize in others and not even know it.

This is kingdom imagination.

I need to challenge myself continually too, on preconceived ideas, judgments, perceptions, and narratives about people. Additionally, I need to have the courage to respectfully challenge people when they express preconceived narratives of other people. It may not change the entire world, but small steps have the possibility of changing us.

For example, what does it look like for you to share a meal with a person you vehemently disagree with on any issue? It might not change your views (or perhaps it might), but it could make you more empathetic. And in the land of a thousand trolls, where we never think we are one but everyone else is, it might help us become more human. It's worth trying to live as a rule of life.

With that mind-set of grace, Emily can hear these raw stories and perspectives. She shared with me about the experience, changing the names of the participants:

> **At the table,** in a room full of strangers, when asked about her thoughts on abortion, Janet says, "I'm an atheist, and a liberal-leaning one at that ... I don't believe God exists. But I've always believed in the sanctity of life. I don't know why, and can't articulate exactly what it is about it, but there's something inside me that refuses to let the innocent die."

> **At the table,** when asked point-blank why he "dared" to vote for Trump, Serge, an immigrant who waited ten years to gain entry into the US, responds, he "would have been on the streets if tax laws continued to rise for self-employed citizens under a different presidency. His health insurance costs were choking him out and left him little to no choice in his presidential vote at the ballot."

> **At the table,** Rowan, who grew up in a fundamentalist Christian home, but turned away from the faith in later years, asks, "Why are Christians so adamant about life being lost in the womb but turn a blind eye to suicide rates and the mental health crisis we face today?"

At the table, when Aja asks Juan directly if he came to the United States legally, Juan tells a story of his ancestors, his young nephews and nieces who've lost their lives crossing the border for the dream of safety. The room is quiet. The question remains unanswered, and a moment of reverence permeates the room.

The essence for any of these dinners is the desire not to teach, or to pick apart what someone might say, but instead to listen purposefully, actively. To be humble to acknowledge that we may have blind spots and to give space for others to have differing views. Don't be lazy and make assumptions about people. Ask about their stories. Then listen. Genuinely listen. Be humble. Be teachable. Be human. Be a good neighbor.

Emily continued:

Active listening is the practice of taking in someone else's words *before* mentally preparing a response, and it is *not* easy. It's the art of sitting in the mud with someone before telling them to get up and move on. Just sitting. Just listening. If we want to be a people who bring hope and healing to a broken culture, with the message of Jesus, we must be willing to scoot over to make room at the table for the untouchables, no matter who they might be.

I love that visual. This is the kingdom imagination we desperately need. Making space for another. Scooting over, sharing a meal, and listening. This takes action and discipline on our part. We cannot sit idly by and wait for the world to come to us, fixed. And when it does … to think exactly like we do.

Let us take this to heart, and not only on occasions like a carefully orchestrated dinner that is designed to spark conversations about faith, politics, and life with neighbors, family, coworkers, and strangers alike. Let us also embody this philosophy of friendship and fellowship with our family and friends—despite how crazy they may be—on both the holidays and the every days. Let's become keen listeners so we can stop tearing others down and be about building the kingdom of God.

WHAT'S ON YOUR HEART AND MIND?

1. "As we challenge ourselves to go deep, to be circumspect, to know the issues, it's also of critical importance to get our noses out of books and media and actually engage with others who don't look like us." Consider the last political conversation you had. Were you talking with someone just like yourself, or someone very different?

2. How well do you know and understand your neighbors, coworkers, or community members? Think of two or three of them, and make a list of their top three political concerns. Can you empathize with those concerns even if they're not your own?

3. Have you ever been in a position like Amanda was, where you challenged the status quo and were ridiculed for it? How did you respond?

CHAPTER 4

THOU SHALT BE ABOUT THE KINGDOM OF GOD

From a prison cell, a man was losing hope as he awaited his likely execution. After hours slipped into days, days became weeks, and weeks piled into months, the faithful evangelist confided in a couple of close friends, telling them his doubts about God. He questioned the core of his faith, the purpose behind his life's work.

John the Baptist, the prophetic voice crying out in the wilderness, became uncertain about Jesus' identity and what He brought about in the world. From prison, John asked two of his disciples to go and ask Jesus, "Are you the one who is to come, or should we expect someone else?"[1] This is particularly noteworthy because if there was anyone who was sure about Jesus, it was John the Baptist—the one whose responsibility was to prepare the way for Christ the Messiah. After all, John the Baptist personally baptized Jesus. Nobody else can ever claim that on their résumé!

John's disciples went on their way, finding Jesus surrounded by people, a large, noisy crowd. Around Jesus were not the rich and royal, but the poor, desperate, and even the demon possessed. They had come to Jesus because they had heard He might be the one to lift the burdens of desolation and sickness from their lives. When they had no other way, they found *the* Way.

Jesus replied to the messengers:

> Go back and report to John what you have seen and heard: The blind receive sight, the lame walk, those who have leprosy are cleansed, the deaf hear, the dead are raised, and the good news is proclaimed to the poor. (Luke 7:22)

Jesus revealed His identity to John through a sermon of His actions. The King of Kings, God incarnate, was with the sick, the hurting, the disturbed—and He was seeing them, loving them, and healing them. He proclaimed who He was by showing examples of His kingdom breaking through.

Jesus had been speaking of His kingdom, but it was so different from what people expected that even the prophet who proclaimed His coming didn't see it. Jesus' kingdom did not appear to be important, but like a mustard seed, it started small and grew into something substantive, strong, and rooted. The value of the kingdom may be overlooked, but it is significant, like a prized possession.

> The kingdom of heaven is like treasure hidden in a field. When a man found it, he … sold all he had and bought that field. (Matt. 13:44)

This was not the King anyone expected, not even the King that John the Baptist expected.

Recall the promise for the Jews as predicted in Scripture, the promise for a spiritual and physical nation, a dream of a King to make things right.

You can see a vision of the King in Psalm 47:1–4:

> Clap your hands, all you nations;
>   shout to God with cries of joy.
> For the LORD Most High is awesome,
>   the great King over all the earth.
> He subdued nations under us,
>   peoples under our feet.
> He chose our inheritance for us,
>   the pride of Jacob, whom he loved.

He is indeed the great King over all the earth, and yet Jesus conducted His ministry in a way that was so different than anyone imagined.

I suspect John the Baptist envisioned Jesus could do what he was doing but on a bigger scale. John might have expected Jesus to rule as many of us would assume if Jesus followed marketing and promotions strategies from our era. Bigger audiences. More sermons. A louder voice with sound effects, strobe lights, and fog machines. Multisite venues with ginormous screens. More miracles and baptisms, etc.

John probably imagined Jesus cracking heads and taking names. The truth is, we are still surprised at how Jesus led, or more accurately, we forget how Jesus led since our natural inclination is to gain and exert power. But this is a different kind of rule, because Jesus is a different kind of ruler and King. With His message back to John, Jesus announced there was a new order breaking in and, with it, a new way of living.

Jesus could have answered John's question in a variety of ways, but He chose to respond in a uniquely Jesus way: by showing the whole gospel at work. Don't get me wrong, Jesus clearly tells people to repent, "for the kingdom of heaven has come near,"[2] and directs people to reconcile with God. Jesus is the Savior of the world. We should never abandon, relinquish, or be timid about sharing that message with the world. But when John asked about the Savior's identity at this moment of crisis, Jesus' answer vividly showed the depth, height, width, and heart of the gospel.

This was the King of Kings who rode into Jerusalem on a donkey, preaching service to others, humility and love for our enemies. A king who welcomed children, who told us "the kingdom of God belongs to such as these."[3] A king who was surrounded by people who needed care this side of heaven, at the time that John the Baptist's disciples found Jesus to ask Him if He was the One.

For those who are hurting and forgotten, Hope has arrived. Hope has come to be with us, to reconcile us to Him, and to change the nature of how we live. This is the fullness of the scandalous and profound beauty of the gospel. This is a gospel that proclaims God's love for all people, including and especially to those who have been forgotten in our society and, dare I say, even in our churches. Love is not nebulous or theoretical. Love serves, washes feet, sacrifices, forgives, embraces the hurting, and welcomes all to the table. This is the gospel lived out.

It's not just about the Four Spiritual Laws or lofty, amorphous theology. Simply put, it is hope for those with no hope.

This is the way of Jesus.

We must recognize that we are both spiritual and physical beings called into a right relationship with God and with our neighbors, the two greatest commandments. How much more can we witness to the kingdom of God breaking through on earth than when we first break into the lives of those around us by loving our neighbors so that God's love can be touched and felt? If we're not all about revealing the kingdom, what are we focused on?

JUST FOCUS ON JESUS?

When I became a follower of Jesus at age eighteen, I had a compartmentalized view about how my faith should animate other aspects of my life. My mind-set was to not care about politics, but to instead "just focus on Jesus," as if it were an either/or choice to be made.

My perspective then, because that was what I was told by more "mature" Christians, was that politics were inconsequential to our discipleship. As an aspiring faithful Christian, I should go to church, serve in the local church, do my devotionals, attend Bible study, and not ask too many questions. Consequently, I didn't care about what was going on in my neighborhood. I didn't care about my city. I didn't care about policy, and to be honest, I didn't even know what policy was about. I didn't care about social justice. But I cared passionately about evangelism.

Though I was never a street preacher exactly, I did occasionally go to the streets to preach or to evangelize. I remember probably a dozen occasions when some friends and I drove from UC Davis to downtown San Francisco to share the good news of Jesus Christ, utilizing a yellow mini pamphlet called *The Four Spiritual Laws.*

When we came upon a homeless person, we'd talk with him or her. I would kneel beside homeless men or women as they sat or lay on the ground, and I would ask them, "Excuse me, if you were to die tonight, do you know where you'd be tomorrow morning?" After they all nearly answered with, "Huh?" I would follow up with, "Do you want to accept Jesus as Lord and Savior?" Not surprisingly, most of the times they would say, "No," or other choice words best not to share here.

I remember so many conversations like this, kneeling to someone sprawled on the ground. I'd get their attention, look into their eyes, and ask if they were saved. There were elements of compassion in this, as everyone needs Jesus. But I am troubled by how compartmentalized my thinking was at the time.

When a homeless person said, "No," I just moved on. It never crossed my mind to ask if they were physically okay, if they were hungry, if they were thirsty, if they were cold, if there were other ways I could help, if they knew any agencies or organizations they could connect with, etc. My perspective on evangelism was focused solely on a yes or a no, and if it was a no, I'd simply move on. My street-preacher moment of life is an example of what can happen if we ignore the effects of society and politics on people simply because they don't have the direct eternal impact of saving souls.

In other words, the kingdom of God isn't merely about a ticket to heaven. It didn't dawn on me until later during Holy Week that Jesus didn't just enter Jerusalem and go straight to the Cross. In between, He confronted corruption and hypocrisy, overturned tables, healed the blind and sick, hosted a meal for His imperfect friends, and washed feet.

The kingdom of God is about life on earth as well as eternity in heaven.

THE NEW THINKING

The kingdom of God is all around us in the beauty and pain of the world. Jesus proclaimed that His kingdom was already here, and not yet to come, a tension by which we await the future glory while being invited into God's redemptive work in the world.

Those who believe only in the "not yet" kingdom are tempted to gloss over or ignore the physical pain around them, waiting for their future glory.

Those who believe the kingdom is already here might discount the need to repent to receive God's grace. They may even expect to lead a charmed life, but Jesus didn't promise any of that. He was not a health and prosperity preacher. No Gulfstream G650 private jet for this king. Instead, He said, "In this world you will have trouble,"[4] and challenged people over and over with the sacrifice needed to follow Him.

> Then a teacher of the law came to him and said, "Teacher, I will follow you wherever you go."
>
> Jesus replied, "Foxes have dens and birds have nests, but the Son of Man has no place to lay his head."
>
> Another disciple said to him, "Lord, first let me go and bury my father."

But Jesus told him, "Follow me, and let the dead
bury their own dead." (Matt. 8:19–22)

Clearly, Jesus never took a class on growing His platform through perks, benefits, monetization, and fluff. This is not quite the kind of sales pitch you can optimize to gain the most likes, followers, and converts. This is a different world of thinking, requiring both our souls *and* our bodies.

We cannot reduce kingdom work into only spiritual or only physical activities. The life of a Christian was not meant to be compartmentalized in this way. As followers of the living God who acts on this earth through His people, we must be reconciled to God, and we must also love our neighbors. And part of loving our neighbors must be caring about the world in which our neighbors live.

The radical kingdom vision should inform and inspire each of us, especially those in authority, to a better way of living. To love God and love people—the great commandments—should have us questioning everything about our lives if we are to fully embrace kingdom living. It's bigger than any political party or political system. It is reimagining the nature of our lives in every way, including how we engage politics, because our political decisions impact our neighbors.

No one has a monopoly on the kingdom of God.

And by no one, I'm also speaking of political parties or political leaders or any other human figure or institution. No matter what the experts, leaders, and polls say. No matter what research, the pope, Billy Graham, Kanye West, Joyce Meyer, Trinity Broadcasting Network, Eugene Cho, or whoever else says. No party or candidate has a monopoly on morality, spirituality, and certainly not on the kingdom of God.

The kingdom of God cannot be contained by our political parties or religious institutions. Thanks be to God for that!

THE NEW RULE

What is the kingdom of God, exactly, and how does it intersect with our lives today, including our politics?

The phrase "kingdom of God" appears 162 times in the New Testament, and not once in the Old Testament, though the ancient writers do occasionally refer to "the kingdom" or "your kingdom" when addressing the Almighty. While I don't agree with late professor and scholar Marcus Borg on significant theological positions, I appreciate how he described the context surrounding Jesus' new paradigm of kingdom living:

> In his world, "kingdom" language was political. Jesus' hearers knew about other kingdoms—the kingdom of Herod and the kingdom of Rome (as Rome referred to itself in eastern parts of the empire). The kingdom of God had to be something different from those kingdoms.
>
> The kingdom of God is for the earth. The Lord's Prayer speaks of God's kingdom coming on *earth*, even as it already exists in heaven. It is about the transformation of this world—what life would be on earth if God were ruler and the lords of the domination systems were not.

If Jesus had wanted to avoid the political meaning of kingdom language he could have spoken of the "family" of God, or the "community" of God, or the "people" of God. But he didn't: he spoke of the kingdom of God.[5]

The theology of the kingdom of God is critical. In short, it illuminates the truth of the reign of God. We believe Jesus came to remind the world emphatically about the kingdom of God. In fact, Jesus represents the kingdom of God through His life, teaching, ministry, healings, and reconciliation. All these aspects give us a glimpse of what the kingdom is all about. The Beatitudes are a beautiful portrait of the kingdom of God, and a couple of them hint at the mind-bending nature of who is prized in Jesus' kingdom:

> Blessed are you who are poor,
>> for yours is the kingdom of God.
> Blessed are you who hunger now,
>> for you will be satisfied. (Luke 6:20–21)

Jesus framed so many ideas and parables through juxtapositions of commonly held positions and beliefs. His life of unconditional love, His challenge to repentance, and His deep personal sacrifice are all an example of the kingdom of God.

Pastor and author Rick McKinley leads a church in Portland, Oregon, called Imago Dei Community—a body of believers called to be an incarnational presence not only in the most desperate parts of world but also in the city. Through a host of ministries including foster care, outreach, and intervention for those impacted by sex trafficking—especially children and refugees—their community is an example of what the kingdom of God can be on earth.

McKinley wrote in his book *This Beautiful Mess* about the nature of the kingdom of God and observed how the kingdom of God is a state of being—not doing—and how that can be frustrating to people like Rick, who (like me) is always driving to accomplish the next good work:

> Pastors and lay leaders love to talk about advancing the kingdom, about building the kingdom. It is as if Jesus said, "My kingdom is a pile of lumber on the truck in heaven, and I need you boys and girls to get a hammer and help Me nail this thing together. Could ya?"
>
> But He didn't. When Jesus talked about the kingdom, He never talked about us building it or advancing it. Never. He said, "The kingdom is …" He simply invited His followers to see it, embrace it, believe in the unfading reality of it—and join in what His Father was already doing in the world.[6]

When we speak about the kingdom of God, it's not some nebulous, distant, romantic, faraway concept. We are not saying someday the kingdom will come to earth as it is in heaven. It's happening … now. God is at work. This truth should inform and influence the way we live our lives. Not to be fatalistic, as in yearning for this to be real once we die, but to be people of hope today—and to love discovering and participating in the kingdom of God. This is contrary to our nature and can be extraordinarily challenging, especially in those moments of life when we are mystified or even paralyzed by the brokenness of the world.

How shall we live in this tension? We are called to be "peculiar people,"[7] as Peter referred to Christians. We are born again, God's possessions, living differently as our lives are being transformed. Though it may be difficult at times, we can take comfort in the fact that God is already at work, and therefore, we must discern how to be about God's kingdom.

LIVING OUT A KINGDOM MIND-SET

Pastor Tim Keller of Redeemer Church in New York said Christians must remain engaged in politics, as nonparticipation is a vote for the status quo. But how does our faith intersect with politics? How do we live out the mind-set of the kingdom? In what way should our faith decisions manifest into legislation?

Keller said, in many ways, it's a matter of practical wisdom. Clearly there are aspects of governance like opposing racism and caring for the poor and oppressed that are clear imperatives for believers. But how, specifically, should our convictions animate into laws? Keller wrote:

> However, there are many possible ways to help the poor. Should we shrink government and let private capital markets allocate resources, or should we expand the government and give the state more of the power to redistribute wealth? Or is the right path one of the many possibilities in between? The Bible does not give exact answers to these questions for every time, place and culture.[8]

In the face of hopelessness, Christians cannot withdraw from their neighbors under the impression that they are unwanted and so grant what they think the world wants.

Michael Wear identified three tangible ways our Christian hope points the way to political hope:

1. commitment—active involvement in pursuing the authentic good of our communities rather than withdrawing into selfish isolation;
2. justice—a firm conviction, expressed in action, that doing right is better than doing well; and
3. humility—overcoming the domineering passions of the culture wars and seeking to be of real use to others rather than to be in charge of others.

Wear continued, "We do not love our neighbor for affirmation, but because we have been loved first. Now is not the time to withdraw, but to refine our intentions and pursue public faithfulness."[9]

As Christians, we cannot pretend we can transcend politics and simply "preach the gospel" if we truly want to love our neighbors and pursue public faithfulness. Jesus did not call us only to be saved; He called us to follow Him—and He goes to some uncomfortable destinations.

We live in a physical reality in which our political action or inaction impacts those around us—our neighbors. And part of the way we care for our neighbors is to respond to the circumstances affecting them.

As Keller said, "To not be political is to be political."[10] American churches in the early nineteenth century did not speak out against slavery because that was what we would now call "getting political."

Because they did not actively pursue justice, they were actually supporting slavery by their inaction.

The ways of the kingdom are not the ways of the world. My theology does not fit in a party platform. No single party represents me and my convictions. Therein lies the tension of trying to discern where my home is. I sometimes feel like an outsider. A fish out of water.

As I see it, we must be flexible in our political leanings but inflexible with the way Jesus taught us to live and love—and that's a lot of tension. A party might claim to be the party of Christ, but no political party fully models the way of Jesus. Not even in polarized pro-life versus women's rights debates.

EQUALITY *AND* DIGNITY

One of the most difficult and heartbreaking issues in our political world today has become a litmus test for the vote of many Christians. Abortion has become a line in the sand for political parties and believers, which is understandable, as it has huge significance. But to me, a pro-life Christian isn't simply about being against abortion. I want to be about life from womb to tomb.

What does being pro-life mean for kids? For immigrants? For the disabled? For groups of people who are often at the losing end of the criminal justice system? For the elderly?

Some progressives forget the womb portion. I felt disturbed when I read about the movement to "Shout Your Abortion," with the leader of the movement wearing a shirt with those words emblazoned across it like a badge of honor. She wants women who have had abortions to proclaim it proudly to show how common it is. Nearly one in four women in America have had abortions, after all.[11]

The goal of the Shout Your Abortion campaign is to destigmatize the procedure.[12] Clearly there is no nuance within this campaign to talk about the deeply disturbing aspects of abortion; it's glossed over. But I also recognize that if you were to change *Roe v. Wade* and outlaw abortion, which would be up to the Supreme Court, it would prompt many questions about how you would legislate and enforce that. I can't imagine prosecuting a single, poor woman for having an abortion, potentially jailing and separating her from her family.

Should there be legislation banning the procedure, or should it only be a deeply personal, ethical choice? Can we change the narrative in America to be neither for nor against abortion? Could we instead be passionate about consistently valuing life, including that of the unborn or pre-born?

The issue of abortion grounds so many to the Republican Party, but for years, America has had time to overturn abortion through Republican presidencies, twenty years of Republicans in control of Congress, twenty years of Republicans in control of the Senate, and years and years of a conservative-leaning Supreme Court.[13]

Jim Daly of Focus on the Family has taken a more pragmatic approach to abortion, engaging with people from Planned Parenthood and the National Abortion and Reproductive Rights Action League (NARAL), the prominent abortion-rights organization. Representatives from NARAL say they want abortion to be "safe, legal, and rare." While Daly can't get behind the idea that an abortion is ever "safe," what more can be done to make sure abortion is rare? Daly wrote in the book *Still Evangelical?*:

As pro-life evangelicals, we might not be able to end abortion outright, but how many babies might be saved in the short-term if we were willing to find areas we can agree on with those with whom we disagree?[14]

While the vast majority of abortions are elective, this isn't simply because of vanity. In many cases, it's driven by a lack of ability to support a child. Half of abortions are among poor women, and increasingly so. What does this tell us? Abortion has become more and more of a procedure of economic desperation, with half of abortion patients below the federal poverty level in 2014 and 30 percent in that same income level about thirty years ago.[15] I continue to have significant ethical concerns about abortion, and always will. But how much could we reduce the incidence of abortion if we invested in resources to make young women more financially stable? Do our politics support that? Do we support these convictions with our personal charitable decisions?

I am deeply passionate about the pro-life movement. I was one of the keynote speakers at the Evangelicals for Life conference held in Washington, DC, in 2017. But because of my personal nuance about *Roe v. Wade*, some evangelicals made it clear that they were unhappy with me as one of the speakers. Despite some interesting emails I received once I was announced as a speaker, it was important for me to be there—and I will continue to speak up for the rights and dignity of the unborn.

Why did I accept the invitation to speak? And why did I participate in the March for Life rally held during the same time frame? Because I believe the gospel doesn't exclude social justice and human dignity.

Because I believe every single man, woman, and child—including the pre-born—is created in the image of God. I believe in the sanctity and dignity of life from womb to tomb. Not only babies' lives, but also the lives of their mothers. Not just our lives, but their lives. Not just American lives, but Syrian lives. Not just Christian lives, but Muslim lives. To be pro-all-life is to acknowledge the systemic injustice that operates against indigenous and black and brown people in our culture. To be pro-all-life is to be broken by the fact that LGBTQ youth are three to six times more likely to attempt suicide.[16] And the list goes on …

While we ought to be clear about the sanctity of life, we must also acknowledge the nuances and complexities. I cannot shame women for a decision I can't even fathom, and I don't support the criminalization of women. Pro-life should not just be an anti-abortion conviction. It is so much more. We have to reduce the demand for abortion and seek to engage policies that reduce that demand or perceived necessity. We must come alongside the poor and low-income women, for this demographic constitutes about 75 percent of abortions.[17] Some will disagree, but we ought to provide access to birth control. We must engage and support those called to foster care and adoption. And in the midst of all this, we must pray for the presence and power of the gospel, pray for hearts to be transformed. And we must love well.

May we elevate and celebrate a culture of life. Not only life itself, but the God who gives us the gift of life and the gift of His Son, Christ.

After the Evangelicals for Life conference, a few wondered how I could have been given a platform to speak there. Eventually, one of the speakers at the event went on to name me in a diatribe on the very popular website Desiring God. It's not pleasant to receive dozens of "You're a baby murderer" emails.

Interestingly, though, I also heard from various individuals and groups associated with progressive Christianity. Many of them shared their utter disappointment that I would agree to speak at such a conference. Thus, I received my share of "You're such a disappointment," mostly anonymous emails like this one:

> Eugene, it's utterly shameful that you're speaking at Evangelicals for Life. In doing so, you are being complicit in a patriarchal and misogynistic platform that devalues the empowerment of women and their God-given freedom to have full and total autonomy over their bodies. As someone that supposedly has been an advocate for women and leadership, I can't comprehend why you would betray women. There is no dignity in the oppression of women. I am so disappointed in you and ask that you'd reconsider.

Following the conference, I was uninvited from several speaking engagements from a few conservative circles, including a couple of churches and college campuses, and told from some organizers that I'd never be invited again to any future progressive events.

While it disappointed some, I also attended the Women's March in Seattle to show my solidarity with my wife, my mothers, my daughters, and the female congregants of my church. I also march in order to model for my son what we believe in our home. Many people have already expressed their disappointment, dismay, and disgust with my decision. They felt that my participation in the march meant I supported the cause of abortion.

Most importantly, I march not because I agree or disagree with every single statement or sign, because I don't, but because as a Christian, I believe in the fundamental truth that women are fearfully and wonderfully made in the image of God. They are to be valued, heard, and respected. And because I believe we can't be a flourishing society without the flourishing of women. Because the church cannot be the church without the gifts and voices of women. All the gifts of women.

To support both the equality of women and the dignity of the unborn feels like a very lonely place to be, but I know I'm not alone. May we press on.

The simple, black-and-white answers to life's difficult challenges might make for a good sound bite, but that certainly does not mean they are the right answers. As I said before, the ways of God's kingdom are not the ways of the world. In the world, we live in a sea of opinions, judgments, and division. But God's kingdom calls us to love our neighbors—all of them—regardless of their beliefs and regardless if our responses fit into neat categories. God's kingdom defies any earthly categorization.

CROSS THE STREET AND LOVE YOUR NEIGHBOR

Many of the most important political decisions are, in fact, local. Here in Seattle, we are dealing with a major homelessness crisis that appears to be worsening. I see people living in cars and in tents in neighborhood parks in a city that is home to Amazon and other prominent companies, and the median home price is $820,000.[18]

It matters who and what I vote for, especially locally, and what happens to my literal next-door neighbor. To care or obsess about national politics while disengaging from local affairs can cause dysfunction in our cities and country. To be uninformed about our home cities' and states' politics is unhealthy for our nation. I liken this dissonance to those who are enamored by global missions or the global poor and yet ignore sharing their faith with their neighbors or coworkers or have no interest in serving the poor in their own cities.

I'm not suggesting that caring for global missions or the global poor is a bad conviction. Obviously not. I travel often to encourage global missionaries and agencies, and as I shared earlier, I founded and run a humanitarian development organization focused on global extreme poverty. Rather, I'm pointing out the disconnect when we're obsessed by the larger world and yet can't even cross the street to build relationships with our very own neighbors. From a political perspective, this is why we shouldn't only engage with national politics, but we must seek to live out our faith in our neighborhoods and communities. By ignoring this invitation, Christians are likely missing out on kingdom work in our own cities.

In the Seattle area, more than twelve thousand people are without a stable place to live. In Seattle and the surrounding county, we have the third largest homeless population in the nation, behind New York and Los Angeles, and the numbers are growing.[19] This breaks my heart. Throughout the many years I've pastored in Seattle, I've grown to know by name many who are homeless or living in their cars on the streets.

Considering the number of unsheltered is growing in Seattle, and that nearly two-thirds of chronically homeless folks struggle with addiction,[20] something significant must happen. Police feel they can't enforce the law concerning public camping because of guidance from city leaders, and the homeless folks couldn't pay fines even if they were levied. So the tents stay in parks and medians. It's frustrating to many people.

Even as we put pressure on local elected officials to provide leadership with this growing crisis, this is an opportunity for local church members to love our neighbors.

In 2010, Quest Church, after years of building relationships and trust, birthed the Bridge Care Center (BCC)—a drop-in center for men and women experiencing homelessness or economic hardship in our neighborhood of Seattle. There, men and women receive a safe, warm place to rest, enjoy movies and snacks, and most importantly, meet with case managers and advocates who can assist with referrals to housing, services, and treatment. At our core, the work we do at the BCC is rooted in dignity. We know that all people have worth. Caring for our community is a collaborative effort in which we bridge connections between our clients and various organizations and services in order to provide sustained support for those struggling and those working to move themselves up and out of homelessness.

While the ministry of the BCC is deeply meaningful, it's also filled with growing challenges. In the past year, our small local ministry engaged with 773 individuals, hosted 4,200 drop-ins, and distributed 24,500 resources to those in need.

We've sought to convene other local stakeholders, businesses, and churches. We've attended many local community meetings. We've met with the mayor of Seattle along with other officials. We've raised significant resources to assist with the homeless, including funding and volunteering in the building of several "tiny homes" for women choosing to leave domestic violence or drug addiction.

Why? Without a government that values each individual—their life, their health, their future—our society will forget those in the margins. And without intentionally valuing all people, our nation or even any smaller community will never live up to its full potential. As Christians, we must heed the Scriptures that we must be particularly mindful of those who are marginalized. Psalm 82:3 urges us to "defend the weak and the fatherless; uphold the cause of the poor and the oppressed."

If we're not willing to cross the street to love our neighbor, we have no right to be enraged at national politics. But if we're about kingdom work in our neighborhoods and cities, we can help to bring about positive change nationally.

WHAT'S ON YOUR HEART AND MIND?

1. What does "being about the kingdom of God" mean to you?

2. How does the kingdom of God intersect with your life today, including your politics?

3. "To care or obsess about national politics while disengaging from local affairs can cause dysfunction in our cities and country." Are you politically involved or about kingdom work in your city? If not, how might you get involved?

CHAPTER 5

THOU SHALT LIVE OUT YOUR CONVICTIONS

In my first book, *Overrated*, I confessed my struggle of being more in love with the idea of changing the world than actually changing the world. One of the hardest things I've ever done was start a nonprofit with my wife, Minhee. In fact, it was not just the two of us, but our entire family sacrificed much in order to launch One Day's Wages (ODW).

The seed that grew within me was planted there by God, by allowing me to see and absorb the pain of extreme poverty. I had read the facts, the history, the philosophy around humanitarian relief and development, but until I went there to meet people and see it myself, I didn't fully grasp the heart around it.

In Burma (also called Myanmar), my eyes were opened to the struggle of so many people on planet Earth. Two moments during this formative trip stand out to me. One was the conversation I had with a leader of a rural village. This community didn't have a name because they were constantly moving from one area to another as they were fleeing from a military junta committed to eradicating their ethnic group. In other words, genocide.

During this trip, I had a chance to visit a makeshift classroom for young children in the village. Imagine about fifteen nonmatching tables and chairs and an overused, scarred, greenish chalkboard. When I walked in, I was instantly drawn to a graphic collage of photos plastered on the chalkboard. I was horrified and repulsed by the images of women, men, and children with missing or bloody body limbs.

Sensing I was disturbed by the photos, my local host invited me to draw near for a closer look. Not wanting to be rude, I reticently walked closer. It was in this moment that he drew my attention to the bottom row of this poster that showed greenish, grayish, metallic contraptions.

"These are land mines. We must teach, children, avoid land mines," he said in imperfect English.

I stood in silence in that moment, attempting to breathe, absorbing the cruelty that humans can inflict upon other humans.

Later that day, I met some of the members of this village, including some land-mine survivors. I also spoke with another of the leaders, who explained that the salaries of the teachers for the classrooms I had visited were $40USD—not per day, per week, or per month … but per year. This isn't a typo. I was shocked to learn that the men and women who were devoting their lives for the sake of these children were being paid $40 per year. That's mere pennies per day.

As I reflected on the trip, I had much to process. I prayed and felt the Spirit pull me to action. My wife and I decided not to simply write a check but to pray about inviting others to join us to start a movement, to inspire others to give so that the world's poorest would have a chance for a better life. To give in order to partner and empower indigenous local leaders. To believe in the beauty of dignity—that every single human being matters and bears the image of God.

The name of our organization, One Day's Wages, comes from the invitation to give your one day's wage, one day of your pay per year, to help alleviate extreme global poverty. That's .04 percent of your income. To launch the organization, Minhee and I felt convicted to donate one year of salary. As a pastor of Quest Church at the time, that amounted to $68,000.

The problem is, we did not have that money saved up for such an occasion. In fact, we struggled to know how we would do it. But because we felt convicted, we stuck to the dream and got creative. We sold things we didn't need, ended subscriptions to services we didn't need, and simplified our lives. Unfortunately, though, after we had scrimped and saved all we could, we still came up short.

One day, out of desperation and a bit of boredom, I posted an absurd ad on Craigslist, listing my house for rent. That would be the house my family and I live in. The offer: $10,000 for 10 weeks. As I was posting the ad, I thought that if some crazy person actually took me up on the offer, it would put us close to the finish line. But no one would pay that, would they?

You know where this is going.

Not long after I posted it, a man from the United Kingdom in town for business saw the ad and decided to stop by. He loved the house and agreed to the terms, with one exception. He said he would need to move in that Friday with his family. Just two days away. Dazed and likely with a bit of terror in my eyes, I said yes.

Small issue. I had not asked my wife about doing this. I do not recommend doing something like this if you care about marital harmony. Minhee was not happy, but God bless her, she rose to the occasion. She and my kids all pitched in to clean up the house and move out within two days. A bit of context: Minhee is a marriage and family therapist, and she now uses that story as an example of what not to do. I'm so proud to have given her such real data and experience for her counseling and lectures.

LEARNING, LEARNING, LEARNING

Now that we are more than a decade into our work with One Day's Wages, I am learning so much about humanitarian development, and also how much I don't know. But one thing I have seen time and time again is the power of convictions lived out.

Two of our kids are out of the house and in college, and our youngest child will soon join them as well. He miraculously grew to be about seven feet tall, at least that's how tall he seems to me, and I believe he eats eleven meals a day. Two kids in college and a hungry young man at home does cost money.

I think that's part of the reason people have resonated with One Day's Wages. We're not billionaires or rock stars (just wannabe K-pop stars). We are evidence that regular people can make a difference. Looking over the arc of my life, I can see how God is merciful and how God provides when we choose to follow Him in faith.

We consider One Day's Wages a movement, not just a charity. We challenge ourselves and others to put their dollars where their convictions are. And we are captivated by the idea that everyday people have the power to change the world. Money raised goes to fund carefully vetted nonprofits, often small organizations based within the countries they serve. The funding from ODW donors powers everything from disaster relief and refugee camps, to clean-water initiatives, to surgeries for kids in war-torn countries, to child-trafficking prevention, to helping build hospitals and investing in local, indigenous leaders.

From the seed money of our family's initial $68,000 gift, more than 20,000 people have resonated with this vision and have donated. Around the world, 674,000 people in need have been impacted. Our initial investment has been multiplied by more than 100, generating more than $8 million at the time of this writing.

Among the amazing stories in this movement is that of three brothers in Minneapolis who have an unusual hobby. The three Bartz brothers, Austin, Trevor, and Connor, have been using the wonders of Minnesota weather to do good in the world for the last eight years. In front of their parents' split-level home, they sculpt massive snow sculptures, all sea creatures. Puffy the Pufferfish. Slinky the Snow Snail. Wally the Walrus. They're so incredible that they've been featured on *NBC Nightly News* and *Ellen*.

With their increased visibility came an opportunity. Why not use the platform to do good in the world? Through their One Day's Wages campaign, they've raised over $90,000 for clean-water projects in Haiti, Malawi, and other countries around the world.[1] Tools of the job now include a harness and crampons, used to scale up the side of a giant snail. While the first sculpture took eight hours, they estimate the most recent one took them seven hundred hours. The Bartz brothers are in their twenties now, but they still get together—for the art, camaraderie, and passion for helping others.

One Day's Wages is a challenge, a conviction I heard from the Holy Spirit, and it didn't necessarily mean I knew this passion was going to be what is now One Day's Wages. But I didn't want to simply put up a Facebook post or a blog entry. My questions were, How do I embody it? How can this inspire others? And as I discerned the Spirit's leading, this meant it would cause a shift in my life, in the way I lived.

Especially in Western Christianity, we are enamored with a gospel that comforts us, but we are rarely drawn to a gospel that disrupts us. The truth is, though, the gospel does both because we need both. There's something dangerous when we are only inclined toward a comfortable gospel. Initially, when we were planning to start the organization, we did not know that we would give up a year's wages and start a three-year journey. As I look back, I am not sure I would have made the sacrifice at the time if I had known how painful it would be. But what has happened is amazing.

When we started the organization, we thought God wanted us to change the world. There is truth to that, and I haven't lost sight of it. But the incredible surprise is that ODW was a means for God to work in us as well. To change us in the process. As Russian author and philosopher Leo Tolstoy once said, "Everyone thinks of changing the world, but no one thinks of changing himself."[2]

When we live out our convictions and act on them in the real world, our beliefs become more personal. We move from proclamations and conversations to maturation and transformation. While our first motivation to act may be a desire to help others, it also becomes a gift to ourselves. Our life satisfaction improves. Our community expands, our bonds grow deeper, our ability to relate to others increases. When we live out our convictions, we show how the gospel that saves is also the gospel that moves and transforms. The world sees that the Jesus who died is also the Savior who dwells in the lives of His people.

As Christians, we can be pastoral, telling people this is God's will. We can be prophetic, proclaiming injustice. But when you dig into and share the issues you intend to act on personally, you deliver the best sermon ever preached. Indeed, the most powerful message one will ever deliver is a faithful life.

One of the reasons Christianity is in crisis is because of the perceived hypocrisy of Christ followers who preach but do not act. We must be careful not to perpetuate the false gospel of perfection. But when there isn't a connection, a genuine humble desire to embody the things we are passionate about, preaching about, that's when we become mere peddlers. We don't need more empty salespeople, in the same way we do not need more jerks for Jesus. We need authentic people, humbly living out their convictions on the left, right, and center.

LIVING IT OUT: THE PASTOR SPY

Loved, admired, and fought over by scholars and biographers, the story of Dietrich Bonhoeffer is familiar to many Christians: the martyr who began life as a pacifist and concluded it as an executed spy.[3]

Born into a nonreligious family in 1906, the young, bookish Bonhoeffer was captivated by the idea of the divine and shocked his family when at age fourteen he announced that he wanted to be a priest. He graduated from the University of Berlin and earned a doctorate in theology before traveling to Spain and the United States, where he did postgraduate studies at Union Theological Seminary.

Even before coming to the United States, Bonhoeffer was greatly concerned about the growing influence of the Nazis in his home country. That concern and his new fascination and affection for the black church in America, which he later referred to as his "great liberation,"[4] altered his theology in ways that would mark his life.

He left and returned again to Germany numerous times over two decades, residing in Britain and in the United States. During one of those returns, his urging that the German church had an obligation to stand against the persecution of the Jews led to a breakaway church he helped form, the Confessing Church. Ultimately, the Confessing Church seminary was shut down by the Nazis and a disheartened Bonhoeffer left for Britain. But his writing continued and flourished, including the seminal *The Cost of Discipleship*, in which he argued prophetically for greater spiritual discipline and "a costly grace."

Returning one last time to Germany, he was deprived of the right to speak publicly or publish, but he found his way into a role in the Abwehr, a German military intelligence agency, where some of the strongest opposition to Hitler existed. He served as a messenger for the small German resistance to some of his British contacts. He became aware of plots to assassinate Hitler and was involved in efforts to help German Jews escape to safety in Switzerland. During this time, he began to question his own commitment to pacifism, believing that the death of Hitler and defeat of Germany were essential for the good of civilization. Eventually, his involvement on behalf of the German Jews led to his arrest, imprisonment, and his execution.

Bonhoeffer's principled resistance would serve as an inspiration to other leaders, including Martin Luther King Jr. and Archbishop

Desmond Tutu. And the debate over who owns the Bonhoeffer legacy would become a long-lasting tug-of-war among liberal and conservative scholars.

LIVING IT OUT: DOWN WITH A SYMBOL OF INJUSTICE

You may remember Bree Newsome as the North Carolina woman who scaled a flagpole outside the South Carolina statehouse and removed the Confederate battle flag at a Civil War memorial, only to be arrested and see the flag reattached shortly after. I look at someone like Newsome, an African American filmmaker, and see someone boldly living out her convictions.

Newsome has made me uncomfortable in the past, as years ago she produced a satirical video about Senator Mitt Romney,[5] a portrayal I didn't think was fair or in good taste. She's an activist and a musician. But Newsome has a story unlike mine. Her family roots go back generations in the Carolinas. And in the Deep South, racial hurt has etched an indelible mark into the souls of so many people.

Up until 2000, the Stars and Bars flew on the South Carolina capitol building, underneath the US flag and the state palmetto flag.[6] In recent years, the Stars and Bars was relegated to a Confederate war memorial nearby.

Some people think of the flag as signifying heritage, not hate, but according to whom? For the vast majority of African Americans, the Confederate flag is understandably inflammatory. It's associated with the way things were. Before civil rights. Before emancipation. Back when people could be owned because of the color of their skin. The Confederate flag hearkens back to the four hundred years of black servitude and injustice in our country.

For Newsome, seeing the Confederate flag on the state capitol grounds in Columbia hit home personally, especially after a white supremacist murdered nine people in an African American church in Charleston.

Newsome told Vox, an American news and interest website whose mission, in its own words, is to "explain the news":

> My ancestors were enslaved in South Carolina. I know their names. This is not something that's abstract for me in any kind of way. I grew up with my grand-mother who was raised in Greenville, who told me about her experiences seeing the Ku Klux Klan beat her neighbor and things like that. The massacre in Charleston brought a refocus on the flag.[7]

The massacre at Charleston's Emanuel AME Church happened less than two weeks before Newsome scaled the flagpole. The white murderer was steeped in racist ideology, pictured in photos with Confederate flags.[8] Upon his arrest and continuing throughout his trial, he was unapologetic for taking the lives of nine people at the church.[9]

For Newsome, her conviction to take action was based on her Christian faith. She prayed and recited the Lord's Prayer as she committed her act of civil disobedience.

"I very much believe that God called me to scale the flagpole that day and I believe that God would bring me safely down. But faith is something that we practice, so even in that moment just praying and staying focused and calling out to God was very important."[10]

It was in 1961, during the turmoil of the Civil Rights Movement, that the Confederate flag was installed on the capitol dome, honoring the one-hundred-year anniversary of the start of the Civil War.[11] But after Newsome removed the flag through her act of civil disobedience, the flag's days on the capitol grounds were numbered.

Newsome climbed the flagpole about a week and a half from the time of the racist, hate-motivated shooting. But the ensuing public controversy after she scaled the flagpole, and the unabashed alignment of the shooter and the Confederate flag and its racist history, gave legislators and Governor Nikki Haley the political momentum to help get a bill passed and signed, removing the flag permanently. All of this happened within a month of the shooting.

I am convinced that the flag would still be flying now had Newsome not climbed the pole and forcefully taken it down, helping set this in motion. People like her lead the way. They are instigators and activists who stir the pot in uncomfortable ways.

You don't have to be on the political left to challenge the status quo. Although we may passionately agree or disagree with them, people like Newsome challenge us to rise up and live out our convictions.

LIVING IT OUT: COMMITTED TO CHILDREN, OURS AND THEIRS

Andrew and Michele Schneidler began their journey of adoption like a lot of other couples—with infertility. And with that, a roller coaster of emotions. When reality set in, Michele knew she had always been open to the idea of adoption. As for Andrew ... not so much. But one day he prayed, "God, I am looking at this thing called adoption in front of me, and if I'm honest, I'd tell You I'm not open to this idea. But I'm open to becoming open to it."

God's answer to that prayer brought three children into their family, the first through an open adoption and the other two through foster-to-adopt programs. That was just the beginning of their adventures. The seventeen years since they brought home their first son, the Schneidlers have surrendered their lives to not only loving, nurturing, and raising their children but so much more. They've committed their lives to finding permanent homes for children in the state of Washington, to ministering to foster parents and adoptive parents, and to expanding their commitment to orphans to a global scale.

Through his law practice, Andrew became aware that many people who desperately wanted to adopt a child, often a child from within their extended family, could not complete the process because they could not afford the legal fees. So he founded the Children's Law Center of Washington (CLCW) and the Permanence Project. He says the CLCW is "what we're called," and the Permanence Project is "what we do." Between 2012 and the publication of this book, the CLCW helped to facilitate adoption and permanence for more than 468 children. His goal is for the CLCW to provide a model for other states to follow.

Michele and Andrew, and Minhee and I recently went on a double date. While we devoured sushi, we reflected on our years of friendship, and Minhee and I expressed the deep awe and respect we had for them. When we first met them several years ago, they had dreamt up a vision to start a conference and community called Refresh—a nonprofit ministry whose two-fold mission was, and is now, "to bring hope, healing, and community to foster and adoptive parents around the country who are struggling to care for children from hard places. To equip the Church with implementing sustainable post placement support so that the orphan care movement continues to strengthen and grow, ultimately resulting in permanence for orphaned and vulnerable children."[12]

Their annual weekend conference began in 2012 with 175 foster and adoptive families and has now expanded beyond Seattle to Kansas City and Chicago with over 2,500 families represented in 2018. I had the privilege of speaking at this conference in both 2016 in Seattle and in 2019 in Chicago, and it is one of the most unique and life-giving experiences I've ever had. I've been amazed at the vulnerability and camaraderie of those who come. And I have never witnessed so many tears among conference participants, and yet, there were so many glimpses of the power of the gospel at work in the lives of these foster and adoptive parents.

For seven years, Michele served as the orphan-care pastor at Overlake Christian Church near Seattle, then in 2018 she combined her ministry experience with her HR and executive-management experience at Boeing, Microsoft, and Milgard to become president and COO of 1MillionHome, a global reunification ministry seeking to return children to their biological families and communities. This is a fancy way of saying she's working to help close down the global orphanage industrial complex by helping reunite orphans to their biological families and helping orphanages reimagine their work:

UNICEF says there are over 100 million living on the streets and over 8 million in orphanages. Building more orphanages is not the answer for these children living on the streets. The innovative strategy of 1MillionHome is to equip partners to convert their orphanages into reintegration centers that transition children home.[13]

The Schneidlers don't know what other opportunities to serve children and foster and adoptive families may be waiting for them, but Andrew shares that he has learned with each new opportunity to say, "God, I am looking at this thing … and if I'm honest, I'd tell You I'm not open to this idea. But I'm open to becoming open to it."

LIVING IT OUT: REACHING ACROSS THE RELIGIOUS DIVIDE

Those of us over a certain age have a personal story about 9/11. We can tell you what we were doing, what we thought, how we felt. In the cultural debris of those terrorist attacks on America, my friend Andrew (Andy) Larsen took a stand against the spike in assaults toward Muslims in 2001, which were nearly eight times higher than the year before, according to FBI data.[14] As a pastor, he responded constructively to the fear, anger, and occasional violence he saw directed toward Muslims in America by taking Jesus' call to love our neighbors.

Andy has been a longtime leader and member of my church, and calls himself a "Visual Peacemaker," appropriate for the ways he uses photography and stories to humanize those we might want to categorize or vilify. Following 9/11, he was pastoring a church and was horrified to see toxic attitudes, indifference, and a lack of understanding growing toward Muslims in America.

"Jesus calls us to a third response, not fear, and not indifference," Andy said. "My Muslim friends know I am a Christian pastor, but when I come to them and want to know them as a fellow human, and approach them with open arms, I get a reciprocal response. This is a human problem, a global problem. If we can't work and be as Jesus calls us to be, we are failing in our calling to Christ and are failing the world."[15]

Thanks to Andy and many others, in the years following 2001, the number of reported assaults decreased significantly. But in the election year of 2016, we spiked again, exceeding the 2001 level. This was the year when a Muslim man named Omar Mateen murdered forty-nine people and wounded fifty-three others in a mass shooting at Pulse, a gay nightclub in Florida, and the Trump administration proposed the so-called Muslim ban.

This is why we desperately need peacemakers in our culture and society, and in the church. In this cause, we need a rekindling of our imagination that goes beyond "for" and "against." Clearly, we must be against certain things that are contrary to God's kingdom, but it also means we can be creative and subversive beyond blanket statements of our opposition.

Having visited both Israel and Palestine on several occasions, I've often received the "Who are you for and against?" question. In this case, "Are you pro-Israel or pro-Palestine?"

Neither. Both. And so some people become frustrated with me. Join the club. While there's pressure to choose one side, I'm ultimately "pro-kingdom of God"—and thus, for peace, truth, justice, and reconciliation.

I'm shocked to meet Christians around the world who don't even know there are Christians in Palestine—and they've actually been there since, umm, the beginning of the Church. It's hard to articulate the weight, fear, and anxiety in the air because of the occupation, both in Palestine and also for Palestinian believers—truly a minority among minorities. I was honored to be there with Bible college students, pastors, activists, and leaders. It was a privilege to preach from the Holy Scriptures, but more so, good to listen to and learn from the indigenous Palestinian church.

During these visits, it's always an honor to be invited to celebrate Shabbat with new Jewish friends in Jerusalem. It is another important reminder that while we don't ultimately share the same faith because of the distinction in how we understand Jesus Christ, there is shared humanity and, thus, a call for mutual love and respect. During these Shabbat meals, I'm moved not only by the songs and prayers to Yahweh, but to hear stories of how they seek to reimagine what it means to love their neighbors.

As I've shared before, we cannot love our neighbors … if we don't even know our neighbors. A rabbi I met in a recent visit to Israel gathers interested members of his synagogue to take them on visits to West Bank, Palestine. After years of building relationships with Palestinians—both Christians and Muslims—he's committed to helping his congregation share and listen in pursuit of common ground. Through these "field trips," Muslims, Jews, and Christians in both Israel and Palestine are meeting people of the "other" groups for the very first time. Imagine living day to day alongside a group of people but never really knowing anything about them or having a single relationship with a person from that respective group.

It is easy to exclude and even hate those whom we don't know. On the other hand, if we follow the example of Jesus, we are to love all. We must pursue it. To seek to know the diversity of life is to see more of God. Life grows richer when we know and love those who are not like us.

Perhaps with knowing our neighbors we will gain a friend today, perhaps even peace. Perhaps not. It doesn't matter. We are called to be faithful in the tension. Even if we don't enjoy an earthly reward, God has an eternal promise: "Blessed are the peacemakers, for they will be called children of God"[16]

A CALL TO BE BRAVE

Sometimes our circumstances intersect with God's desire for us to love our neighbors. Often when we choose to get involved in kingdom work, we are surprised by the conversations, the relationships. One of the most powerful things we could do is to choose what Jesus did.

Jesus broke bread with people who did not always think like Him or agree with Him. Nowadays, we rarely have meetings around tables like those of Make America Dinner Again. Instead, our conversations happen in online forums. And we have highly contentious neighborhood town-hall meetings.

We can do better. We can be better. I don't want to say, "Just suck it up." But let's not have online outrage be the final say. That cannot be our last song or the totality of our actions. The world needs more than that.

I am thankful Rosa Parks was outraged, but I am more thankful that she did not simply stay an outraged woman. She did not whine and become despondent in her home. She decided to move, to act, to not give up. After many death threats, Martin Luther King Jr. wondered if he should quit. Who wouldn't? Was it worth it? But he persisted. As it so happens, a bomb actually did go off, and thankfully no one was hurt.

We need more of this courage in our world today. Let's not be jerks, but be informed, live out our convictions as followers of Jesus, and keep pursuing the kingdom of God here.

A REAL AND CONVINCING GOSPEL

Christians, this is of paramount importance. As polls have shown, and as you have probably experienced yourself, the world is skeptical of us. People outside of the faith community look at Christians, and evangelical Christians in particular, with suspicion. We are characterized as judgmental and tribal, defined by what we are against rather than what we are for.

This is not the way of Christ. The Jesus I follow is not the emperor arriving on a chariot, but the humble King arriving on a donkey. The all-powerful Lord who chooses a different way, who comes to serve. The Jesus I follow made deliberate efforts to get to know and befriend those who were shunned by society. The Jesus I follow did not have a home, and challenged people to not follow the law, but to live into a new life, a new way of thinking, to bring forth the kingdom of God on earth as it is in heaven.

People around the world universally find Jesus someone to emulate because of the way He lived His life. His words are challenging, but His actions are indisputably inspiring. Of course, I would challenge anyone to look closer at Jesus, to not only respect Him as a teacher, but to realize that He is God's own Son, the Savior who came to redeem us, to give us hope and a future.

As Christians, we must take personal responsibility for living fully into God's call to love our neighbors, whether they be right next door or across the world. As far as I'm concerned, if they are a person, they are your neighbor.

From Matthew 22:

> "Teacher, which is the greatest commandment in the Law?"
>
> Jesus replied: "'Love the Lord your God with all your heart and with all your soul and with all your mind.' This is the first and greatest commandment. And the second is like it: 'Love your neighbor as yourself.' All the Law and the Prophets hang on these two commandments." (vv. 36–40)

WHAT'S ON YOUR HEART AND MIND?

1. With so many issues to be concerned about in the world, which one tugs at your heart most? How strong is your conviction to do something about it?

2. If time and money were no object, and you knew you couldn't fail, what local or global issue might you try to resolve?

3. What is the first step you would take to resolve the issue?

CHAPTER 6

THOU SHALT HAVE PERSPECTIVE AND DEPTH

I urge Christians of all backgrounds and ages to go deep in their knowledge and convictions in order to gain perspective and depth concerning political involvement.

Come along on a journey with me as we challenge some of what we know about Scripture, persecution, the political dynamics of Jesus' time, and some American heroes—Christians of one variety or another—whose stories are a bit more complex than is commonly known. If we actually understand the why behind our convictions, we'll be more committed to actually living out our convictions—and able to defend them in times of trial.

One of the greatest privileges I've had in my life was to be invited by Rev. Dr. Martin Luther King Jr.'s family and the King Center to speak at the 2017 MLK Service at Ebenezer Baptist Church in Atlanta, Georgia. It was the most beautiful and inspiring six-hour church service I never wanted to end. In addition to preaching a mini-sermon, it was special to be able to meet and speak with Dr. Bernice King (Martin Luther King Jr.'s daughter) and Dr. Christine Farris (his sister).

During a meal together, I learned that "the church" was home base for MLK and many in the Civil Rights Movement. Whenever possible, it was where Dr. King and others met before and after rallies, marches, and protests as both a symbol of safety and empowerment. A reminder of who they served and why they were pursuing justice.

Today, everyone seems to want a piece of Rev. Dr. Martin Luther King Jr. He is universally loved in our modern era, with an approval of more than 90 percent of Americans.[1]

Everyone wants to claim him as their own, whether they are on the left, the right, or smack-dab in the center. If you don't believe me, simply go to the next MLK march in your respective city and you'll notice organizations, clubs, and special-interest groups with their respective signs with MLK's unauthorized endorsements of their causes and issues.

How could you not like quotes like these? Imagine these words in a white sans-serif font, superimposed over a rugged mountain landscape, then shared on your social-media platform of choice:

"Darkness cannot drive out darkness: only light can do that. Hate cannot drive out hate: only love can do that."

"Our lives begin to end the day we become silent about things that matter."

"Faith is taking the first step even when you can't see the whole staircase."[2]

And consider these statements from the two major political parties in the United States:

"Through nonviolent activism Martin Luther King, Jr. altered the course of American history," said former co-chair of the Republican National Committee Bob Paduchik one MLK day. "May we remember and cherish the things he held dear and treat one another with dignity and respect, today and every day."[3]

"As we celebrate Dr. King's life and legacy, we must recommit ourselves to the same principles he and so many other heroes have fought for: justice, equality, and opportunity for all," said Tom Perez, chair of the Democratic National Committee, on another MLK day.[4]

Even Ram used a quote from Dr. King to sell pickups during a Super Bowl commercial.[5] Remember that?

MLK challenged the authorities of the day, despite the culture of bigotry and the personal bigotry of America's leaders. President Lyndon Baines Johnson couldn't help himself from calling black people the *n* word even as he signed landmark civil-rights legislation.[6] And yet MLK challenged Johnson and worked with him. MLK was committed and never gave up.

MLK pulled from his deep well of morality and integrity and stood firm to ideals that could stand the test of time.

But was that all there was to Martin Luther King Jr.? Did you know he was wildly unpopular during the Civil Rights Movement of the 1960s, with a 75 percent disapproval rating the year he died? He was far more than a grandiose, forward-thinking pastor. MLK was also countercultural. A rebel. A radical. Unpopular, and increasingly so was his activism—and then he was assassinated.

While many are aware of the quotes that regularly show up on social media and of his famous speech, "I Have a Dream," I'm shocked by how little people know of MLK, the seminary-trained preacher. In fact, on several occasions, I've met people who had no idea at all that Dr. Martin Luther King Jr. was also an ordained minister.

And if you didn't know that, you might not fully appreciate how absolutely radical he could be. He protested the Vietnam War and once said, "We've committed more war crimes almost than any nation in the world."[7]

MLK was also critical of many aspects of capitalism, including the resulting economic inequality. He once criticized advertisers, specifically those who try to persuade us to buy cars we might not need because of our fallen human instinct to stand out in front of the crowd.[8]

Does anyone see the irony with his voice being used to persuade folks to plunk down $60K for a Ram 1500 Limited? To be fair, the ad was alluding to the idea of using their pickups to serve others. But still, I'm not sure MLK's passion was for a 5.7-liter V8 Hemi.

The manipulation of MLK is significant, but I expect it's one glimpse into how all of us need to examine what we believe, and why.

My advice to you as you seek to engage politics more intelligently: gain some perspective and depth. Don't just be a headline reader. Be educated. Learn. Go deep.

Voters, and especially people of faith, must realize that political parties and candidates may distort, manipulate, cajole, emotionalize, tug, and use whatever other tactics to "speak" to our faith. And if we're not careful, we can be dumbed down and influenced in such a way that a candidate's strategic use of "Christianese" becomes the dominant or even the only factor in determining our vote.

PERSPECTIVES ON PERSECUTION

Many American Christians are responding in fear to the idea that we are under attack by the enemy. There is a concern that our way of life is in jeopardy. Muslims are evil and out to get us. Gay people are out to get us. The New England Patriots are bad and out to get us. Our good, Christian people are being sidelined while our Christian nation is unduly influenced by other religions and liberalism.

In the book *A People's History of Christianity*, author Dr. Diana Butler Bass speaks of "Big-C" Christianity, which is "a theological disposition that interprets Christianity as an us-against-them morality tale of a suffering church that is vindicated by God through its global victory over other worldviews, religions, or political systems."[9]

This is the Christianity of territory and conquest—the kind of militant Christianity that "tolerates (and often encourages) schisms, crusades, inquisitions, and warfare as a means—metaphorical if not actual—to the righteous end of establishing God's will on earth."[10]

American Christianity has become more like this Christianity, an expression of cultural Christianity rather than kingdom of God Christianity—the kind of incarnational, loving Christianity that drew so many regular people to countercultural Jesus, to the frustration of the Pharisees, who eventually plotted to kill Him.

We have become more concerned with conquering America for Christ rather than loving as Christ loved, speaking truth, and showing people the way to Christ through word and deed. The Christianity the next generation longs for has existed before, but it seems so uncommon in America today.

Dr. Bass calls this kind of faith "Great Command Christianity" and talks about the power of emulating the good Samaritan, to "go and do likewise."[11]

With our mind-set of protectionism, Christians in America end up worrying about the wrong things, or at the very least, we spend a lot of time fretting about a few issues, while not focusing on the kind of faith lived out that could truly proclaim the kingdom of God.

I'd love it if everyone was Christian and said Merry Christmas, but I realize that not everyone is Christian. Frankly, if my faith was dependent on whether someone said Merry Christmas, that wouldn't be much of a faith at all, would it? Rather than being so obsessed with keeping Christ in Christmas, we ought to be more concerned about keeping Christ in Christian. If God extended free will to people, who am I to force my faith onto others?

Is the ultimate goal to build an island for ourselves, walled off from society, with all the political protection we can muster? As we read in Mark, "What good is it for someone to gain the whole world, yet forfeit their soul?"[12]

Christians, we do not need to center our faith, politics, or emotions on these social hot-button issues. And let's not waste a moment with positively menial stuff, like getting up in arms about the design that appears or does not appear on Starbucks cups at Christmastime. The work of the kingdom is bigger than a grande macchiato. Let's think twice before we protest graphic designs on paper cups. (Although, I did feel persecuted once when a barista spelled my name Eugenie.)

I do not want to minimize the instances in which Christians are being treated unfairly in America, but when we fight about relatively minor problems here, we are doing a disservice to our Christian brothers and sisters who are indeed under attack in other countries, including Baptist pastor Chu Yiu-ming in Hong Kong, a brave hero of the faith.

Pastor Chu and eight other activists were convicted for crimes related to their involvement with pro-democracy groups. At the time of this writing, he faces up to seven years in prison, and others with additional convictions could spend more time behind bars. True freedom is "more than loyalty to the state," Pastor Chu said, and he believes that each person has potential and can make a contribution to society.

The seventy-five-year-old pastor told the courtroom in Cantonese:

> "We have no regrets. We hold no grudges, no anger, no grievances. We do not give up," he said, speaking on behalf of fellow activists involved in a campaign to bring universal voting rights to Hong Kong. "In the words of Jesus, 'Happy are those who are persecuted because they do what God requires; The Kingdom of heaven belongs to them!'"

He went on to say:

> "The seeds of peaceful non-violent civil disobedience action have been planted deep in the heart of Hong Kong people," Chu said in his testimony, which led some supporters to tears. "This movement is an awakening of the civil spirit.… Wellbeing, decency, and peace constitute our common dream. It is also the will of God. Let us strive to make it real for our city."[13]

This is a dangerous time globally to be a Christian, and in terms of the number of people involved and the gravity of the crimes committed, "the persecution of Christians is today worse than at any time in history."[14] The nonprofit Open Doors helps and advocates for persecuted Christians and estimates that 245 million Christians face high levels of persecution. 245 *million*. That's one in nine Christians worldwide. India and China, the two most populated nations in the world, now rank on the top ten of the organization's "World Watch List," a barometer of both physical violence against Christians and the day-to-day pressure they feel while living out their faith.[15]

The number one most persecuted country for Christians on the list? North Korea. The home of my ancestors, and the former "Jerusalem of the East." My friend Pastor Kenneth Bae spent more than two years there at a labor camp, and he now runs a nonprofit called Nehemiah Global Initiative to serve North Korean refugees. The stories he tells of his time there, and the stories other men, women, and children tell, if they've managed to find their freedom, are chilling. It's also rare to hear an account from a Christian there, because Open Doors notes that if the authoritarian government discovers a Christian in the country, that person is sent to a labor camp, or even killed on the spot.[16]

The Catholic organization Aid to the Church in Need says North Koreans face "unspeakable atrocities," including enforced starvation and abortion. The organization has heard reports of Christians hung on crosses over a fire, and others being crushed under a steamroller.[17] The repressive communist state fears what could happen if people learned that their hope and savior wasn't named Kim Jong-un.

Are Christians under attack in America? In some cases, yes, and we can be mindful of that. But let's not be deceived by culture-war rhetoric that Christians are under widespread attack in America and conclude that the worst persecution is here. Often, American Christians can become so caught up in thinking people are out to get us that we root our politics and voting decisions in fear. In other words, we end up voting "against" instead of "for" candidates and issues. Don't just vote for what you're against. Show us what you're about. Create a better story. Compel us. Invite us. Help us reimagine a better story.

ALWAYS RESPECT AUTHORITY, USUALLY

Most of us have been taught we shouldn't disrupt the status quo, and we're supposed to respect authorities. One of the most cited passages in Scripture that supports this belief is in Romans, but a deeper look shows it's not as simple as we've assumed it to be.

Paul was writing to Christians in Rome who lived in an oppressive, anti-Christian environment, a hostile time to say the least. Nero had just become emperor, and while Paul likely was not yet aware of that development, he would have known that Roman rulers were persecuting and exiling both Christians and Jews. Nero was just the most colorful of the motley crew. Lions, dogs, human torches for his gardens. Lots of bad stuff.

It's a bit of a mystery how Paul could write to these people and say in chapter 13:

> Let everyone be subject to the governing authorities, for there is no authority except that which God has established. The authorities that exist have been established by God. Consequently, whoever rebels against

the authority is rebelling against what God has instituted, and those who do so will bring judgment on themselves. For rulers hold no terror for those who do right, but for those who do wrong. Do you want to be free from fear of the one in authority? Then do what is right and you will be commended. (vv. 1–3)

Peter offered a similar admonition in 1 Peter 2:13–16:

Submit yourselves for the Lord's sake to every human authority: whether to the emperor, as the supreme authority, or to governors, who are sent by him to punish those who do wrong and to commend those who do right. For it is God's will that by doing good you should silence the ignorant talk of foolish people. Live as free people, but do not use your freedom as a cover-up for evil; live as God's slaves.

Former US attorney general Jeff Sessions used the Romans passage to defend a policy of separating illegal-immigrant and asylum-seeking parents from their children at the US border:

First—illegal entry into the United States is a crime— as it should be. Persons who violate the law of our nation are subject to prosecution. I would cite you to the Apostle Paul and his clear and wise command in Romans 13, to obey the laws of the government because God has ordained them for the purpose of order.

Orderly and lawful processes are good in themselves and protect the weak and lawful.[18]

Others have used it as a "gotcha" passage or a hammer to defend slavery, the American Revolution, those who opposed the American Revolution, the list goes on. It's not a new phenomenon.

Conversely, author T. L. Carter, with substantial support from ancient texts, has posited that Paul was using the rhetorical device of irony, which would have been patently obvious to those who received the letter, less so to us two thousand years later.[19] Have you ever written an email or sent a text that would only make sense to the person receiving it? Me too.

Even without the ancient texts, a case can be made that the issue of respecting authority and following the law—all laws, no matter what—is more complicated than Sessions and the slave owners would have us believe. At least twice, in Acts 4:18–19 and Acts 5:27–29, Peter was one of the apostles who stood in the face of authorities and told them he would obey God rather than governing authorities and would continue preaching about Jesus.

But for those who would use these passages as a hammer to justify all kinds of disobedience, civil and otherwise, we must recall that Peter was not opposing an inconvenient law, or even an unjust one, but rather one that stood diametrically opposed to the instruction he had received from God.

Jesus told His followers to pay taxes to Caesar. One could argue that those same tax dollars were used to pay the Roman soldiers who oversaw crucifixions. Yet He said, "Give back to Caesar what is Caesar's, and to God what is God's."[20]

The only laws we actually know Jesus broke were those that would have forbid Him from healing on the Sabbath, and for allowing His disciples to reap grain on the Sabbath. Perhaps in His admonition to the Pharisees who objected to plucking heads of grain, we find the key to solving this dilemma:

> The Pharisees said to him, "Look, why are they doing what is unlawful on the Sabbath?"
>
> He answered, "Have you never read what David did when he and his companions were hungry and in need? In the days of Abiathar the high priest, he entered the house of God and ate the consecrated bread, which is lawful only for priests to eat. And he also gave some to his companions."
>
> Then he said to them, "The Sabbath was made for man, not man for the Sabbath. So the Son of Man is Lord even of the Sabbath." (Mark 2:24–28)

All three synoptic gospels record that story. Must have been important.

Now let's look at a few stories of American heroes of faith and justice, not to give you an authoritative take, but to reveal some inspiring elements of their stories and to challenge ourselves to go deeper.

HARRIET BEECHER STOWE

Harriet Beecher Stowe was born in 1811 and learned as a young American woman that while she could not vote, could not hold public office, and was discouraged from public speaking, she could make a difference with her words. She was a genius artisan of writing, with an insight into the soul of the nation.

Stowe's father was a minister and later a theology professor who encouraged his children to engage in lively debates at the dinner table. He expected his children to shape the world around them. Her brothers became ministers. One sister founded the National Women's Suffrage Association, and another pioneered education for women. Stowe wrote *Uncle Tom's Cabin*.

She was forty when she wrote it, initially as a serial for an abolitionist newspaper, *The National Era* published by Gamaliel Bailey. Stowe expected to write three or four chapters, but after a lot of prodding, she kept writing … eventually completing forty chapters. The book was translated into twenty-three languages and sold more than one million copies, second only to the Bible as one of the bestselling books of the nineteenth century.

Uncle Tom's Cabin brought Stowe's family the financial security it lacked on the humble minister's salary her husband earned. More significantly and poignantly, it helped start the war that ultimately ended slavery.

Harriet met Abraham Lincoln in 1863, who reportedly told her, "So you're the little woman who wrote the book that made this great war!"[21]

Nancy Koester, a Lutheran pastor and professor who wrote *Harriet Beecher Stowe: A Spiritual Life*, has said that while Stowe was known by many as a literary figure, "what drove her literary production was her Christian faith."

"The religious aspect of her life was a wellspring for the rest of her life," Koester said.

Some have called *Uncle Tom's Cabin* more of a sermon than a novel, and Koester agreed. The book "tried to convict people of slavery as sin, convert them to an anti-slavery position, and then set them on a path to bring slavery to an end."[22]

YU GWAN-SUN

Almost no one in North America knows about Yu Gwan-Sun, and that's understandable. Even most Korean Americans have limited knowledge of this nonviolent freedom fighter. Yu Gwan-Sun was born in 1902 to Christian parents in a little village near Cheonan, Korea, and at sixteen years old, she was one of the thirty-three activists who gathered together to read a declaration of independence on March 1, 1919. This date and event are often considered as the rise of the Korean independence movement from Japanese colonial rule (although full Korean independence wouldn't arrive until August 1945).

While it would be erroneous to isolate the Korean independence movement to one person, it would also be a mistake to diminish Yu's significance. By 1919, most political Korean groups had been forcefully disbanded by the Japanese government, which made this uprising that much more shocking to both the Japanese government and the Korean people. The movement began, in essence, with primarily young students and Christians, and Yu "became the face of the nation's collective yearning for freedom."[23]

While most Koreans know her as one of the primary figures of the Korean independence movement, many might gloss over the significant role her faith in Christ played in her life, activism, and leadership. She was deeply influenced by both her Christian parents and American missionaries who sympathized with the movement. She and her family worshipped at a nearby Methodist church where she memorized many Bible verses. Eventually, American missionaries encouraged Yu to attend Hakdang Mission School for Girls in Seoul and, later, Ehwa school (another school for women established by American missionaries) to further her education.[24]

What began with a handful of students declaring independence on a day in March quickly grew to hundreds and, over time, thousands. Within several weeks, approximately two million people throughout Korea (out of a population of twenty million) had participated in 1,542 pro-independence marches.[25] Tragically, the Japanese government grew brutal in their attempts to quash the protests, which led to many people dying and even more being imprisoned. Sadly, among those killed were Yu's parents, and Yu herself was imprisoned and tortured. She later died due to her injuries in 1920, at the age of seventeen.

While the world rightfully equates Mahatma Gandhi and Rev. Dr. Martin Luther King Jr. to the subversive power of nonviolence as protest, such actions from Yu actually preceded theirs. Yu's legacy included her commitment to mobilize thousands of Koreans, other Christians, and to fight for justice and independence through her call for peaceful protest and nonviolence.

SOJOURNER TRUTH

Sojourner Truth was born Isabella Baumfree in 1797 to slave parents in Ulster County, New York. Between the ages of nine and thirteen, she was sold three times, and though she fell in love with a slave on an adjacent farm, she was forced by her owner John Dumont to marry one of his slaves.

In 1826, after Dumont reneged on a promise to free her on July 4, she took her infant daughter, left her other children behind because they were still Dumont's property, and walked away, eventually making it to New Paltz, New York, where she and her daughter were taken in by Isaac and Maria Van Wagenen. Dumont tracked her down, but the Van Wagenens purchased her services until the New York Anti-Slavery Law emancipating slaves took effect a year later.

While staying with the Van Wagenens, Isabella became a Christian and eventually moved to New York City, where she worked in succession for two different evangelists. Her life among fellow Christians emboldened her, and she ultimately changed her name to Sojourner Truth and followed a call to evangelize and to preach against slavery and oppression both of slaves and of women.

Some abolitionists, including Frederick Douglass, believed black men were more worthy of full rights than black women. Sojourner Truth was adamant in her opposition and, from that platform, delivered her most famous speech, widely referred to as "Ain't I a Woman?," at the Ohio Women's Rights Convention in May 1851. The most reliable transcript of that address concludes:

> I can't read, but I can hear.
> I have heard the bible and have learned that Eve
> caused man to sin.
> Well if woman upset the world, do give her a chance
> to set it right side up again.
> The Lady has spoken about Jesus, how he never
> spurned woman from him, and she was right.
> When Lazarus died, Mary and Martha came to him
> with faith and love and besought him to raise
> their brother.

And Jesus wept—and Lazarus came forth.
And how came Jesus into the world?
Through God who created him and woman who
　　bore him.
Man, where is your part?
But the women are coming up blessed be God and a
　　few of the men are coming up with them.
But man is in a tight place, the poor slave is on him,
　　woman is coming on him, and he is surely
　　between—a hawk and a buzzard.[26]

EMMETT TILL

Emmett Till was just a fourteen-year-old kid from Chicago visiting cousins in Mississippi when he was accused of flirting with a white woman, Carolyn Bryant, who was a checker at a grocery store owned by her husband. Four days later Till was kidnapped by the woman's husband, Roy Bryant, and his friend J. W. Milam, taken to a barn in the middle of a cotton field, and beaten brutally while black sharecroppers listened from outside. When the beating was done, he was shot in the head, lashed with barbed wire to a discarded fan blade, and thrown into the river.

Emmett Till was just a kid. A kid who became a martyr. His mother was the hero who made his name and life the catalyst for the American Civil Rights Movement.

Over objections of Mississippi officials who wanted the body buried quickly, Till's mother, Mamie Till-Mobley, insisted it be returned to Chicago for a funeral. Then she requested that the casket be opened to reveal the body of her child, so disfigured by the beating and decomposition that he had been identified only by the initials on a signet ring she had given him before he got on that train from Chicago to Mississippi.

When she saw her son's body, she demanded that the funeral be open casket. And it was. Depending on which account you read, between 50,000 and 100,000 people passed by that casket. In an un-air-conditioned August, they waited for hours outside the church. Some fainted.

Bryant and Milam were acquitted by an all-white male jury that deliberated sixty-seven minutes. All juries in Mississippi were all white and all male in 1955. Black men and all women were not allowed on juries. One sharecropper testified, but it didn't matter.

Bryant and Milam confessed to *Look* magazine a few years later. Many years after that, Carolyn Bryant admitted she had lied about what happened in the store that day.

But Emmett Till was still just fourteen years old. And dead.

Only a month after Emmett's funeral, Mamie Till-Mobley began speaking often about her son's death. She was committed, determined, and zealous that he had not died in vain. The words she used frequently, "died in vain," echoed not only those of Lincoln at Gettysburg but also Scripture. She claimed to have had a vision that compelled her to be sure her beloved son's life and death made a difference:

> I was angry with God that He had let Bo [her nick-
> name for Emmett] be kidnapped and slain so brutally
> and aloud I demanded, "Why did You do this [?]" ...

Then began one of the strangest experiences of my whole life. It was just as though someone had entered the room and we were carrying on a conversation …

The presence said to me, "Mamie, it was ordained from the beginning of time that Emmett Louis Till would die a violent death. You should be grateful to be the mother of a boy who died blameless like Christ. Bo Till will never be forgotten. There is a job for you to do now …"

"What shall I do?" I asked.

The voice replied, "Have courage and faith that in the end there will be redemption for the sufferings of your people and you are the instrument of this purpose. Work unceasingly to tell the story so that the truth will arouse men's consciences and right can at last prevail." The Voice died away and the Presence left the room.[27]

Eight years to the day after Emmett Till died, Martin Luther King Jr. spoke on the steps of the Lincoln Memorial. In the interim, Rosa Parks refused to give up her seat on the bus. Medgar Evers, who investigated Till's death for the NAACP, was murdered. The Greensboro sit-ins began. The Freedom Riders. The Birmingham Campaign. The Children's Campaign. Riots. More. And all of them knew about Emmett Till because his mother had opened his casket and listened to the voice of God.

A CALL TO BRAVELY AND PRAYERFULLY DISCERN

The stories I have shared are accounts of the lives of imperfect people following the call of God, the same God of Micah 6:8. He is the God who through His prophet instructs us to walk humbly and seek mercy—but also act justly. Part of acting justly means we must prayerfully discern times when we should respect authority and also discern those times when we should defy the ways of the world. The Spirit is at work, after all. If we are sensitive to being in the Word, and sensitive to the ways of the Spirit, we may find ourselves forging a new God-inspired path for living, a more just path for all. The heroes of the faith, the faithful believers who helped write the first draft of history, did not stand idly by. God's truth and values guided them. Though their journey might have been difficult, even costing them everything, God showed them a better path, a far better road than the rough trails designed by man.

WHAT'S ON YOUR HEART AND MIND?

1. What is your view on the persecution of Christians in America (or your country)? How much does your view influence your political conversations and voting?

2. Read Micah 6:8. How does the Bible's instruction in that passage inform your political views?

CHAPTER 7

THOU SHALT NOT LIE, GET PLAYED, OR BE MANIPULATED

I've been duped before. Misled. Tricked. Fooled. Manipulated. Or if I'm honest, I've *allowed* myself to be misled and manipulated. In our culture today, we should be much more discerning and wise, especially because truth seems so much murkier.

When it comes to politics, do you remember the first time you were misled or tricked? Lied to? Manipulated? For me, while not the first instance, the scenario that comes to mind was when I saw an image of 2012 Republican presidential front-runner Senator Mitt Romney seated and getting his shoes shined by an anonymous man in a bright red jacket uniform.

Accompanying the photo was a brief commentary about this wealth and privilege—and how out of touch Romney was. I didn't know much about him, so the description and the photo sure made Romney unlikable and, well, out of touch. That was my judgment and conclusion.

Then another photo emerged just a couple of hours later on the internet. This time, it was the photo above placed side by side with a photo of President Barack Obama (then seeking renomination) fist-bumping Lawrence Lipscomb, a custodian who worked in federal offices as part of the AbilityOne Program (a federal initiative to help people who are blind or have other significant disabilities find employment).[1]

But the awkward truth was that the Romney photo wasn't what it was described to be at all. In actuality, Romney was at the airport on a tarmac getting his shoe wanded for security purposes like other passengers—not shoeshined.[2] The man in the bright red jacket uniform wasn't a shoeshiner but rather a TSA security agent. The juxtaposition was clear: Romney was wealthy and privileged, and Obama was humble and accessible. Eventually, the Romney photo began to spread like wildfire through the internet, and people were duped, misled, tricked, and fooled.

Why?

Because that's the nature of politics. It can get nasty and while not all, many people have agendas. If we're not careful, we can easily be duped, misled, tricked, fooled, manipulated, and we can easily spread lies and half-truths to others, both unknowingly and, even worse, knowingly.

Ever since that shoe incident, I vowed to be careful and be certain to never make a similar mistake again—except that one time ...

OUTRAGE AND JUDGMENT

It was an image and video seen repeatedly on social media and the national news in January 2019. A crowded, chaotic scene with lots of teenagers at the National Mall, just a short distance from where Rev. Dr. Martin Luther King Jr. delivered his "I Have a Dream" speech more than fifty years ago.

In the scene, high school junior Nick Sandmann, a smiling young white man from Covington Catholic High School wearing a red Make America Great Again (MAGA) hat, stood inches away from the face of an older Native American man named Nathan Phillips. Phillips was singing and beating a drum. All around him was a crowd of young white men, many wearing the same Trump-campaign hats and smiling, shouting, and laughing. They had just attended the anti-abortion rally March for Life, and Phillips was just leaving the Indigenous People's March. Phillips was vastly outnumbered. He appeared to be trapped, as if the young men had surrounded him.

A snippet of video, a few photos, and a quick interview with Phillips, and the mainstream media and social media quickly grew enraged. The headlines included: "Teenagers Taunt Native American Elder in Washington"[3] and "Students in MAGA Hats Taunt Indigenous Elder, Demonstrators in Washington: VIDEO."[4]

As a person who cares deeply about justice, and seeing what I saw, I quickly drew the conclusion that a smirking kid wearing a MAGA hat, staring down a Native American man, was in the wrong. Clearly this young man and his classmates were seeking to bully and intimidate Phillips. I believed that these white students of privilege, from a private school, were intimidating an older, indigenous gentleman and taunting him.

I took to Twitter and to my fifty thousand followers and made a stand for justice, right along with thousands and thousands of others. I then cross-shared it on Facebook to my nearly forty thousand page followers. I raised my voice to call out the apparent wrongdoing. It felt both good and right to address what was disgusting and painful to see.

The problem was, I was wrong. I didn't see the full story. It wasn't as simple and clear-cut as I initially thought. Most of the media didn't catch it either, which helped color my viewpoint. Even Sandmann's school didn't see it, as they issued a statement soon after the encounter condemning the actions of the students.[5]

But in the days that followed, the story grew more complex and nuanced. I learned that immediately before Sandmann and Phillips stared at each other, members of a group called the Black Hebrew Israelites were nearby, taunting the students with homophobic and racial slurs. The students did not respond in kind, and Phillips felt compelled to get in the middle of the whirlwind with his song and drum to ease tensions. So that meant Phillips moved into the group of students instead of the students surrounding him. And though a lot of video was being shot at the time, there's no proof that any student from the Catholic school said, "Build the wall."[6]

And how about the Twitter account @2020fight that posted the video that helped fuel the outrage? It showed just a fraction of the footage, without context, and was later suspended by Twitter for "deliberate attempts to manipulate the public conversation on Twitter by using misleading account information." The account may have been run by a California teacher, tweeting on average 130 times a day, and has since been deleted.[7]

I began to rethink, reexamine, and eventually regret my quick social-media proclamation of injustice. In short, I realized I had made a mistake, and in hastily engaging the frenzy of social media, I had also misled those who followed my accounts. And for the sake of integrity, I needed to apologize.

Here's some of what I wrote in my apology:

I saw a video over the weekend involving Native American activist Nathan Phillips and numerous students from Covington Catholic High School. By now, many of you have probably seen it or heard about it. I watched the short clip three times and each time, it grieved me—for many reasons. As someone who deeply cares about decency, justice, mercy, and highlighting people, spaces, and places of injustice, I posted a brief commentary and shared this short video clip on Facebook and Twitter.

Now having watched more of the much longer video and having read additional commentary from others, it's now very clear to me that while the students of Covington are not completely innocent, they did not initiate or instigate that moment as I first believed and judged. It's also clear to me that Nathan Phillips did not seek to fuel the already intense situation because I believe him when he shared that he entered that space in order to diffuse brewing tensions and continue his prayer. I still believe we have much to learn from him and that we need to make space for indigenous people as a whole. It's clear to me that the situation was way more complex and contextual than I believed and conveyed to others.

Now, I have many additional thoughts about the situation like respect, mocking, cultural appropriation, etc. ... but that's not the purpose of this note. This is an apology. It's my apology.

What's most clear to me is that I was wrong, and I have to take responsibility ... for my irresponsibility ... in sharing the video without taking the proper and necessary time to more fully understand the situation. Sometimes, in my passion for confronting injustice, I can accelerate the listening and learning process and that's simply dangerous and ironically, something I've often encouraged others not to do. (Umm, I wrote an entire chapter about this in my book.) I made that mistake here.

As I was processing this situation, I was surprised that I first began to justify my mistake because I was busy, hurried, and rushed—which is precisely why I should have paused and refrained.

So, I want to take this moment to publicly apologize to the students of Covington. I mailed a letter this morning to these students in hopes that they might personally receive it.

And I also need to apologize to those who follow me on social media. I was wrong. I was foolish. And I apologize and ask for your forgiveness.

During these crazy and chaotic times, I sincerely believe it's important to engage our culture, confront evil, humbly speak truth, and seek to pursue God's kingdom—as messy as that process may be. With how the internet works nowadays, I'm fully aware that most will likely move on to the next thing and people would likely forget not only this news but also likely dismiss or forget my post but as we urge leaders and influencers to take responsibility, we can't do that if we're not willing to do that ourselves. It feels—at least to me—that we have so many definitive statements and declarations … and so few apologies.

This is my apology.

Thanks for reading and considering it.

Do we need to speak up? Of course. Sometimes, we absolutely do. But sometimes we don't. Sometimes we probably do but we need to wait for more information to know for sure. A temptation of our culture is the need to debate and comment on every single event. Sometimes, wisdom is evident in silence. Sometimes, silence is necessary for sanity. It's okay. Let someone else win the internet.

As much as possible before we speak up, let's make sure we're getting the full story and not just seeing a facet of it—or worse, not falling for some preposterous conspiracy theory. Before we share, we need to make sure we're not becoming a pawn in a misinformation campaign. Before we get riled up, let's make sure we really understand. In our culture today, we have to resist the temptation to be the loudest, the angriest, and often, the first to speak or last to speak in an effort to get the first or final word.

A CALL TO CIVILITY

As human beings, it's inevitable that we will disagree, but not just on political issues. People are simply going to disagree. I love my wife immensely and we don't agree on everything. I love my church and we don't agree on everything. But what seems to be increasing in our polarized culture is not merely a desire to win an argument but to shame, crush, or destroy the opposition.

My call for civility is not a call for a sterile lack of engagement. It is to engage while extending the human courtesy of respect and, dare I say, even wanting others to flourish. To engage and not lose our souls in the process. Civility and kindness are not substitutes for peace and justice. My call for civility is to reject the notion that one needs to be a jerk in order to seek peace and justice. One can engage in civility *and* pursue justice. We can do both.

The progress made in the Civil Rights Movement in the 1960s was made possible partly by the passion of the people seeking equality as well as the reason behind their fight. It also was made possible by the way the fight took place, through repeated, determined, nonviolent events. A nonviolent movement goes against our human inclinations, and with convictions, it embodies the kind of behavior God expects. It's almost supernatural. It seems divine.

Nonviolence means that we will not return evil for evil. It means we will turn the other cheek. We will love our enemies. And yet it does so bravely, leaning forward into the conversation no one is allowing us to have—and speaking up for matters of justice. For matters of equality. To make things right that are broken. Nonviolence is not an invitation to be trampled on. Rather, it requires us to believe that God's ways are more powerful than ours. And that's why it works, at least in the long term. God designed us, and He knows how radical it is for us to put down our weapons and instead seek to manage the task at hand with clear eyes and conviction.

Turmoil and deception are tools of the evil one. We are guided by the eighth commandment, to not bear false witness against our neighbor, and we are called to be light and truth by Christ—to love God and to love our neighbor.

Additionally, the enticement we feel toward outrage and half-truths has an impact not only on the receiver but also on us, if we are the person stating the lie. When we knowingly lie, attack, or sin, we harm other people and ourselves. This is the nature of sin.

Even worse, when we are in the cycle of lying and deception, we begin to have a hard time discerning truth from lies. We may even begin to believe the lies we tell. This affects not only our relationships with other people, but it certainly affects our relationship with God.

GETTING PLAYED AND PLAYING OTHERS

The story of the Catholic students and the Native American man, and how it was widely interpreted and misinterpreted, is a microcosm of a plague we seem to be comfortable with.

In our partisan, fragmented society, where everyone has access to a megaphone through social media, we often use our megaphones to project lies or half-truths. Sometimes it's unintentional. Sometimes it's intentional. Sometimes it's because we're lazy. Sometimes what we say and do is intentionally vindictive in order to push the narratives we want others to believe.

Regardless of all the reasons we do or allow these things, this is a problem. As Christians, we should be concerned about this new societal norm. We have heard the command to not bear false witness, but so often we share or believe information of dubious value.

One step we all can take is to simply slow down. If your thumbs have become overly muscular because of scrolling, scrolling, and scrolling on a smartphone—you know what I am talking about. We quickly consume great volumes of information, and not all of it has merit. A significant part of our lives is spent online, twenty-four hours per week.[8] How do we make judgments when we must evaluate thousands of bits of information every day?

An MIT cognitive scientist named David Rand found that, on average, people are inclined to believe false news at least 20 percent of the time.

But when we resist snap judgments, we are harder to fool. "You just have to stop and think," Rand says of the experiments he has run on the subject. "All of the data we have collected suggests that's the real problem. It's not that people are being super-biased and using their reasoning ability to trick themselves into believing crazy stuff. It's just that people aren't stopping. They're rolling on."[9]

We share and retweet links without clicking on them. We depend on search-engine rankings to determine credibility. And very often— we give credence to what we *want* to believe.

We choose to believe cable-news media and social media, often trusting it or sharing it because it affirms our viewpoints or feels good to us. This concern does include news that is indeed false but, more commonly than that, also is extremely partisan and unfair content. Simply doing something because it feels good to us or our tribe is selfish.

We have a huge responsibility now, as the power of media has come firmly into the hands of individuals. We see the benefit of this, with the power of regular people using social media to stand up against oppressive regimes in the Middle East. The power of social media is amazing for fueling ideas and initiating movements.

Make no mistake, this is a powerful shift, and with it comes responsibility. Armed with a smartphone, each one of us has become a journalist, and good journalists tell fair and complete stories. But when a journalist doesn't do their job and gets it wrong, a decent news director will hold that reporter to account. With social media, everyone is their own news director, but without formal training. We have our own agenda, the attention span of a goldfish, and a smartphone camera that always seems to be pointing toward our own face.

No wonder we have a hard time agreeing on issues and candidates.

EMPIRES OF PARTISANSHIP

It may have started with the Drudge Report, birthed in 1995 as an email gossip newsletter with Matt Drudge himself aggregating stories from other sources. By 1997, Drudge had started a website to supplement his $10 per year email newsletter.

Over twenty-five years, other right-wing megaphones have come along, each predicted to threaten Drudge's supremacy, his existence, but it hasn't worked out that way.[10] In 2012, Drudge announced it had hit one billion page views per month, within respectable distance of the *New York Times* at that point. That same year, Business Insider estimated that even if the Drudge Report generated only $1.50 per 1,000 pages, it would be generating revenue of $15 to $20 million a year. It may not sound like a lot in the world of corporate media, but the Drudge Report is a famously lean operation, and one can assume almost all of that goes straight to the pocket of Matt Drudge.[11]

By July 2016, the Drudge Report moved into second place on SimilarWeb's top US Media Publisher rankings, with about 1.47 billion page views. That put it just behind MSN and ahead of news sites like Disney Media Networks (which includes ESPN.com and ABCNews.com), Yahoo, Google, Time Warner, and Fox Entertainment Groups.[12]

Or maybe it started with Roger Ailes.

When Roger Ailes started Fox News in 1996, no one thought he could succeed against CNN. Ailes disagreed. "I built this business to throw off a billion dollars in profit," Ailes told the *New York Times*. "That was the goal from Day 1. In my own mind."[13] Within fifteen years, in 2010, Fox News would earn $700 million in profit, more than CNN, MSNBC and the big three evening newscasts combined.[14]

Or perhaps it started with Rupert Murdoch.

It's not possible to understand the maelstrom of outrage that has come to define American media and the partisan websites, cable networks, and social media that masquerade as news organizations without understanding the role of Rupert Murdoch. In April 2019, *New York Times Magazine* published an epic investigative piece that spanned three continents, more than 150 interviews, and six months of work by the *NYT* team led by byliners Jonathan Mahler and Jim Rutenberg. Perhaps no paragraph ever written summarizes Murdoch's impact better than this one:

> The Murdoch empire did not cause this [right-wing populist] wave. But more than any single media company, it enabled it, promoted it and profited from it. Across the English-speaking world, the family's outlets have helped elevate marginal demagogues, mainstream ethnonationalism and politicize the very notion of truth. The results have been striking. It may not have been the family's mission to destabilize democracies around the world, but that has been its most consequential legacy.[15]

It's critical to understand that while Murdoch and Ailes both hewed to the populist side of politics, they were not initially Trump fans. Murdoch had known Trump for years. They were friends of sorts.

But when first approached with the idea of Trump as a presidential candidate, Murdoch reportedly didn't look up from his soup.

Ultimately, however, they could not resist the Trump ratings. Fox News' entire prime-time lineup changed over a relatively short period of time. Opinion hosts were the ones drawing ratings. Sean Hannity joined a tour for Trump, appearing onstage at a Trump rally in Cape Girardeau, Missouri, and called the other media "fake news." Such behavior by any anchor from any of the other networks at any point in history would have resulted in immediate dismissal. Hannity's star only continued to rise.

Fox stood by Tucker Carlson in back-to-back controversies in late 2017 and early 2018, insisting that no revenue was lost even when more than twenty brands stopped advertising on the show after Carlson said immigration made the country "poorer and dirtier and more divided."[16] Ad inventory was shifted to other programs. Network backing is not surprising given that Carlson's show generated almost $30 million in the first quarter of 2019, second among network shows and representing roughly 14 percent of the network's total.[17]

Fox is not the only one to benefit from talking-head outrage and the "Age of Trump." In 2016, CNN's average daytime audience was up more than 50 percent and its prime-time audience up more than 70 percent. The network earned nearly $1 billion, the most profitable year in CNN's history. Some of that is because of yet another media genius in the form of Jeff Zucker. But CNN was struggling before Zucker, who created *The Apprentice* for NBC, refocused on candidate Trump.[18]

Professor Jeffrey Berry of Tufts University has called this phenomenon the "weaponization of the media." While denser on the conservative side, both sides have it, and it largely attracts the folks he identifies as "high-octane voters," the people who are deeply interested in politics and vote disproportionately in primaries.[19]

Avoid being played and manipulated. Don't feed into the frenzy. Be aware of how information can be positioned and weaponized, and reevaluate your news sources. No network or online news source should be your sole source of information, and realize that fear and conflict help keep viewers engaged and the ad revenue flowing.

OBJECTIVITY, ANYONE?

Reporters are not held in high esteem today, unfortunately. You might remember when Montana Congressman Greg Gianforte body-slammed a persistent reporter who was asking about his position on healthcare.[20] Weeks later, Gianforte was reelected, and Trump said that anyone who can body-slam a reporter was "my kind of guy."[21] Around the same time, Trump refused to punish Saudi Arabia for murdering journalist Jamal Khashoggi and faced backlash from fellow Republicans.[22]

At President Trump's rallies, crowds openly boo members of the press, and Trump openly criticizes reporters. At one rally, he once chided Russian president Vladimir Putin for allegations that he's had journalists killed, saying, "I would never kill them, but I do hate them. And some of them are such lying, disgusting people."[23] Some will read these criticisms and think I've been too harsh, but my intention is to convey the unprecedented nature of the tension surrounding journalism.

And while President Trump didn't coin the term "fake news," he did popularize it.[24]

What is fake news? It's come to mean anything from inaccurate or slanted reporting to dismissing news that does not suit us.

Members of the media certainly get stories wrong, so the criticism of fake news does have merit. The five-time Emmy Award–winning journalist Sharyl Attkisson, who has worked for news sources including CNN, CBS, PBS, and now right-leaning Sinclair Broadcasting, has documented ninety-three media mistakes so far during the time Trump has been in office. The stories span a wide range, including a *Time* magazine story about Trump removing the bust of MLK from the Oval Office (it's still there) to a ProPublica story about Trump's pick to lead the CIA being in charge of a secret prison and mocking the suffering of a prisoner who was waterboarded there (neither claim was true).[25]

President Trump has been known to lie. By the account of the *Washington Post*, he has publicly made false or misleading claims more than nine thousand times since coming into office, currently averaging nearly twenty-two lies daily.[26] But his behavior should not reduce the need for the media to pursue the truth and report accurately.

When people argue about the news, the words "objective" and "opinion" get thrown around with great authority, typically illustrating that somebody has little understanding of either. Newspapers are even criticized for sharing opinions—on their opinion pages. Yet those with the loudest critiques often turn to online "news" sources that are essentially commentary absent of any reporting at all.

Objectivity in journalism is largely an American invention. It arrived on the scene in the 1920s for commercial rather than purely noble purposes. Those who imagine it to be a doctrine rooted with the Founders' commitment to freedom of expression should take a look at the Federalist Papers or at Ben Franklin's *Pennsylvania Gazette* or *Pennsylvania Chronicle*, which was known for its anti-British sentiments. The first American newspapers were all about sharing strong opinions.

Throughout the nineteenth century, newspapers provided views on topics of the day. But early in the twentieth century, as newspapers closed and were merged, the masthead that survived suddenly had to appeal to a larger and more diverse readership. Overt partisanship that might have appealed to the smaller audience in the previous circulation area wasn't going to cut it in the new, expanded area. So, objectivity was born.

The result was often criticized as reducing journalists to stenographers. "They simply reported what powerful people said and did, without providing context or analysis. As the famous radio commentator Elmer Davis noted in 1953, that kind of objectivity 'lets the public be imposed on by the charlatan with the most brazen front.'"[27]

Beginning in the 1960s, more and more journalists included analysis and interpretation in their reports rather than "just the facts." Failing to do so only meant the source with the biggest, flashiest, sexiest, or most emotionally evocative bullhorn would be reported verbatim, even if all the bull was, well, you know.

Journalists came to understand that professional reporting also required professional interpretation and context. "The mayor said this today, but last week he said something different." Pointing out the difference is not lacking in objectivity but essential context to understand what happened today.

The idea of liberal bias in the news can be traced to 1969 and two speeches given by Vice President Spiro Agnew, who later resigned in disgrace and was subsequently convicted on a single felony charge of tax evasion. Agnew had become the media-bashing voice of the Nixon administration as it did battle with the *Washington Post*'s and other major media outlets' coverage of Watergate.

Murdoch's Fox News was seen by some as the counterweight to liberal-leaning "mainstream media." But Fox's alignment with conservative voices, particularly Donald Trump, led many to demean its "fair and balanced" slogan, which was dropped by the network in 2017 in favor of "most watched" and "most trusted."

Indeed, Fox is among the most trusted news sources by its own viewers. But an analysis for Research Intelligencer by Brand Keys in July 2018 found that the BBC—not an American news organization— had the highest trustworthy rating among news sources at 90 percent, followed by Fox News at 87 percent and PBS at 86 percent.[28] The problem with such surveys is that often they measure trustedness, not trustworthiness. If erudite and sophisticated listeners love the British accents on BBC and the eclectic documentaries of PBS but not Fox, and Fox's mid-American conservative viewers trust Fox but not BBC or PBS, what's a well-intentioned news consumer to do? Don't both groups deserve to trust a trustworthy source?

The 2018 Poynter "Media Trust Survey" found that across the political spectrum, 76 percent of Americans do trust their local TV news and 73 percent trust their local newspapers. But only 55 and 59 percent trust national network news and national newspapers, respectively, and 47 percent trust online-only news outlets.[29]

One reason may be that engagement with news is on the rise. The Edelman "Trust Barometer," an annual survey, found that "in 2019, engagement with the news surged by 22 points; 40 percent not only consume news once a week or more, but they also routinely amplify it. But people are encountering roadblocks in their quest for facts, with 73 percent worried about fake news being used as a weapon."[30]

So how can Christians who want to be wise as serpents and harmless as doves know who to trust, know what is fake news, what is false information, and what is not news at all? The American Press Institute has identified six questions (and a host of follow-up questions paraphrased here) to help news consumers know who to trust:[31]

1. Type: What kind of content is this?

Is it a news story or an opinion piece? Is it an ad or what some people call native advertising produced by a company? Is it a reaction to someone else's content? Where does the organization get its money? If it's a nonprofit or an advocacy group, where did that money come from? If that isn't clear, that's a problem. Does the content have an obvious political slant? Usually you have to read more than one story to figure out that last one. If all the stories seem to have the same slant, it's not a reliable source.

2. Source: Who and what are the sources cited and why should I believe them?

Who is being cited? Is it a police official? A politician? What party? If it's research, what organization produced it and what background, if any, is offered about it? Who paid for the research? What credentials does the source have? How close was this person to the events in terms of time and distance?

3. Evidence: What's the evidence and how was it vetted?

Was it a document? A report? Do authorities agree on the conclusions? How many authorities—thousands or a half dozen? Is there corroborating evidence? These things indicate the reporter asked the follow-up questions required to substantiate information and claims made by sources.

4. Interpretation: Is the main point proven by the evidence?

What conclusions are being drawn? Do they follow logically from what has been cited? Are too many conclusions being drawn from evidence that doesn't support all of them? Does the other side get a fair hearing? Does the news source add new information when it becomes available?

5. Completeness: What's missing?

Are there obvious unanswered questions? What can you do with the information? Do you understand the point better and also understand what you can do about it?

6. Knowledge: Am I learning every day what I need to know?

These are the questions you need to ask yourself about whether you're being a wise consumer of news. What do I hear people talking about that I wish I understood better? Where could I go to learn? Could I explain this situation to someone? Look at top stories on a website or a newspaper front page. How many of them are you familiar with? How well do you understand them?

A healthy society needs leaders from various perspectives. In the United States, we need healthier Democratic and Republican parties. We need healthier third parties. We need healthier news reporting. As such, we ought to invest in news rather than blindly consume it. We need to support good journalism locally, nationally, and globally. I don't believe a news source can be entirely unbiased, but I try to seek those that are less biased and intentionally read news from different sources. Not just American news, but world news as well. We can share "news" from entities that are obviously partisan, or even originating from troll farms, simply because we do not take an additional two minutes to conduct cursory research about the media entity.

Swiss theologian Karl Barth lived during the rise of the Third Reich and confronted the Nazis' attempts to create a "German Christian" church.[32] Barth knew the importance of a free press, one that reports with fairness and clarity, but he also knew that in order to properly navigate the world, we must be rooted in the Truth.

Barth was quoted in *Time* in 1963:

> Newspapers, [Barth] says, are so important that "I always pray for the sick, the poor, journalists, authorities of the state and the church—in that order. Journalists form public opinion. They hold terribly important positions. Nevertheless, a theologian should never be formed by the world around him—either East or West. He should make his vocation to show both East and West that they can live without a clash. Where the peace of God is proclaimed, there is peace on earth is implicit. Have we forgotten the Christmas message?"[33]

If we're to be objective, we must always approach the world with both eyes open.

YOU ARE THE GATEKEEPER

We have a growing cultural mantra to challenge and protest others. In my sphere, it is an expectation to rally against injustice. We are against those people doing those things, whatever those things may be. Don't get me wrong, it's often absolutely merited. But we must look inward also. We must take responsibility as well.

I have noticed that many people can no longer challenge members of their own tribes. I see this in politics. Dubious ideas arise that people on the extremes come to love, and more moderate people feel like they must adopt these positions, even if they will never be passed and even if they are not palatable for the greater good. It becomes my way or the highway, and remember, if you're not with me, you're evil.

We must consider how we tend to align politically and then question our tribes. But more than that, this must be personal. We must be willing to pick apart what we believe. We must think independently. We must pursue truth. We must watch what we believe and what we share.

Without this critical thinking, we do not know our blind spots. We begin to believe lies, including our own. We don't see the world with clear eyes. We are alienating our neighbors. We're missing our chance to actually learn and listen. We're missing our chance to grow.

It's our responsibility to be informed. But even as we acknowledge the importance of news and media, we must not live our lives entirely online, always wading into controversies. We can learn so much more from real relationships, so we must be intentional to know our neighbors, and specifically to know and listen to our neighbors who don't look like us, think like us, or vote like us. To engage with people in real life is to have a chance for real life transformation.

Well-informed citizens rarely get played or manipulated. That's not fake news. It's just plain good advice.

WHAT'S ON YOUR HEART AND MIND?

1. Have you ever bought into "fake news," then later discovered the truth? How did that make you feel?

2. Have you ever shared "fake news" with others only to discover that you helped perpetuate a lie? What could you have done to avoid being manipulated by false reports?

3. How can you best avoid being played or manipulated in the future?

CHAPTER 8

THOU SHALT PRAY, VOTE, AND RAISE YOUR VOICE

As Christians, we should all agree that prayer is a good thing. It's not just good; it's a God thing. It's a gift God gives to us, not merely to come to God with our requests, petitions, thanksgiving, and supplication, but also to be reminded that we're connected to God. We need God. To be reminded of our need for God, in itself, is an answer to prayer rather than prayer being a way for us to manipulate God. First Timothy 2:1–2 gives us some clear instructions about prayer:

> I urge, then, first of all, that petitions, prayers, intercession and thanksgiving be made for all people—for kings and all those in authority, that we may live peaceful and quiet lives in all Godliness and holiness.

These are convicting words because Paul clearly understood the political context of the times when he wrote these instructions to

Timothy. They were challenging days for Christians as they endured through misunderstandings and even persecution. And yet, we're instructed to pray—even for those in authority.

My friend James (not his real name) has quietly taught me much about Paul's instructions to Timothy on prayer. James and I are different in many ways. He's a bit older, Caucasian, Catholic, lives on the other coast in the United States, and roots for the New England Patriots. Ugh. We first met through a mutual friend and over the years have enjoyed growing in our friendship. While we share faith in Jesus, we've learned that doesn't always translate into having the same views about many things, including politics. But because we've built our friendship, our trust allows us to ask each other tough questions about why we believe in what we believe.

James has a commitment to pray "for kings and all those in authority." He first started praying for Jimmy Carter when Carter assumed the presidency in 1977—specifically because he was distraught that "one of those Democrats" became president. Ever since then, James has made a commitment to pray for both the president and his respective city's mayor every single day. *Every single day.* He's able to recall specific prayers he's prayed for Carter, Ronald Reagan, George Bush Sr., Bill Clinton, George Bush Jr., Barack Obama, and Donald Trump. He's never missed a day.

When I asked him why he prayed every single day for both the president and his mayor, I was convicted by his words:

> Eugene, I pray for them because Jesus is my Lord and God's Word is my lamp unto my feet. Even if I don't like what I read in the Scriptures, I take it to heart. And so,

I pray for wisdom, integrity, protection, and guidance for those in authority. But over the years, I learned that I needed to engage in this discipline not just for them but … also for me. Praying for them every single day helped humanize them for me … and also made me more human. It has helped soften some of my hardness, anger, or cynicism that I began to feel against leaders that I didn't like or disagreed with. It reminds me that they're people just like me, created in God's image, with fears, insecurities, and hopes. It reminds me that they also need Jesus and, most importantly, that Jesus loves them. And finally, praying for leaders reminds me that my trust is not in human authority, which is why I don't pray to them … but rather, to Jesus.

I'll never forget that conversation with James, and since then, I've taken up the practice of praying for the current president and my mayor. Okay, I may have missed a couple of days here and there, but little did I know that I would actually get an opportunity to pray, on separate occasions, with my mayor and the president of the United States.

PRAYER WITH THE PRESIDENT

Some years ago, I met President Obama while he was visiting Seattle. In my mind, I had envisioned the opportunity to share some heartfelt convictions that would dramatically impact President Obama and alter the trajectory of his leadership, presidency, and country. Go big or go home, right?

Unfortunately, the chance for a long conversation wasn't to be. If I'd had that opportunity, I was hoping to talk policies, justice, human dignity, womb to tomb, family, marriage, compare pictures of our kids, and challenge him to a one-on-one basketball game.

However, the meeting was a few minutes in a small group. When folks were introduced at this smaller gathering, they all had "important" titles. I was simply introduced as "Eugene Cho," and I'm certain many were asking, "Who is this and why is he here?" In fact, President Obama himself had a puzzled look as he said, "Hello, Eugene." So, I introduced myself to him and explained that I was a pastor in Seattle and was also involved with humanitarian work through One Day's Wages. We chit-chatted briefly about stuff, but there is something I remember specifically, and I doubt I'll ever forget this portion of our conversation—even and especially if I disagree with him on certain policies.

I shared with President Obama that I occasionally but regularly prayed for him, and he responded, "Thank you, Pastor Eugene. I really appreciate that. Can you also please pray for my wife and children? Pray for their protection."

His demeanor changed. Perhaps I overanalyzed all the nonverbal cues, but then again, I'm a pastor and after (then) twenty-one years of doing ministry, you develop a "pastoral sense." I genuinely sensed his gratitude for prayer and his request for prayer for his family.

Even now, I vividly remember that short conversation along with a sense of the burden and weight of his job and the "calling" of the presidency. In many ways, we ought to commend the courage of all those who step into leadership—on any level, including the highest. We can criticize them and their decisions, but we ought to commend them also for their courage to place themselves in such vulnerable positions.

Prayer for others is a great antidote to mean-spirited hearts. It doesn't matter what your political leanings, affiliations, and affections may be. We so often quote 1 Timothy 2:1–4 as an encouragement to pray for our leaders but yet hesitate or neglect those instructions when it's someone we disagree with. Sadly, some might start quoting Psalm 109:8 instead:

May his days be few; and let another take his office. (KJV)

This was the inappropriate encouragement of Republican Senator David Perdue of Georgia at a conservative Christian event regarding President Obama.[1] As you can imagine, a great deal of brouhaha erupted because that verse is literally about "may his days be few" … as in death. And then there are those ridiculous and dangerous stories like that of Pastor Wiley Drake, who shared very publicly that he was praying for the death of President Obama.[2]

As the president and I shook hands and shared this brief conversation, I was reminded that despite his being arguably "the most powerful man in the world," beneath it all was simply another broken and fallen man with doubts and fears—just like me. All of us are in desperate need of the grace of God. We're all in need of the comfort and strength that come through prayer. Our brief conversation reminded me of the words I had heard from President Obama himself when I attended the 2011 National Prayer Breakfast in Washington, DC:

And like all of us, my faith journey has had its twists and turns. It hasn't always been a straight line. I have thanked God for the joys of parenthood and Michelle's willingness to put up with me. In the wake of failures and disappointments, I've questioned what God had in store for me and been reminded that God's plans for us may not always match our own short-sighted desires.

And let me tell you, these past two years, they have deepened my faith. The presidency has a funny way of making a person feel the need to pray. Abe Lincoln said, as many of you know, "I have been driven to my knees many times by the overwhelming conviction that I had no place else to go."

It's because of that experience, along with the wisdom and example of James, that I made a commitment to pray regularly for the president of this country. Whoever it may be. Agree or disagree. Like or dislike. Republican or Democrat. Tea Party or Coffee Party.

And so, I pray for President Trump almost every day. If I'm honest, it's often challenging, but I am committed to being respectful of him. I pray for physical protection for him and his family. For wisdom and for repentance too, because all leaders need both. I pray for a deeper sense of compassion—especially for the vulnerable—in our country and around the world. I pray for his well-being, for his marriage and family. I pray for strength, conviction, and courage. I pray foremost that he would know Jesus in a deep, profound way that alters his outlook on self, society, and life. I pray for his commitment to honor God in his life and through his leadership.

Why does prayer matter? It reminds us that we desperately need God in our lives but, additionally, that we're connected to one another. In short, prayer is the ultimate antidote to our propensity to dehumanize and vilify others.

WHEN POLITICIANS PRAY TOGETHER

Despite the ongoing tension in our politics, we can count on one time of the week when our congressional leaders will come to a bipartisan agreement. Wednesday mornings, when it's time to pray. Every week that Congress is in session, two simple prayer breakfasts draw senators and congressional leaders from across the political spectrum, one for the House, one for the Senate. Don't expect to get an invitation to either of these meetings. They are successful because they are private.

Usually about a quarter of the Senate shows up for its prayer breakfast, and it's not a time to talk politics necessarily. Like any successful small group of believers, sharing life and reflecting on Scripture are central to building trust and spiritual depth. Senators and the chamber's chaplain are the only attendees, and the chaplain leads the singing.

Though Republicans generally outnumber Democrats, one democratic senator who faithfully attends is Chris Coons of Delaware. Like former senator Joe Biden, he commutes into the Capitol by train from Delaware every morning, and extra early on Wednesday mornings. Between the train and a walk to the breakfast, he may miss half of the meeting—but even that is a refreshing few minutes.

> "We're all strangers here. None of us belongs here or lives here," says Coons, a Presbyterian who holds a master's degree in ethics from Yale Divinity School and who sometimes guest-preaches on Sundays at various churches in Delaware. The prayer breakfast, he says, "helps humanize this place."[3]

The breakfasts include speakers from diverse faiths, attempting to represent the various political and religious backgrounds. Coons says the breakfasts are a time when people across the aisle actually listen and provide a moderating influence on the division. They share struggles. They share faith journeys and doubts, celebrations and moments to mourn. Friendships built here in study and prayer have led to relationships formed, and bipartisan legislation produced for the good of the country. Once a year, the breakfasts combine, and the National Prayer Breakfast is held.

As Coons puts it, "If you hold hands with someone in prayer in the morning, it's tough for [that] someone to throw a punch at you in the afternoon."[4]

Yup. Don't be jerk. Don't throw a punch. Pray for one another.

THE LONG JOURNEY TO THE BALLOT BOX

"I voted." It's the simple sticker you've probably worn many times. I love these stickers. They are a badge of honor in a country where we are strongly encouraged to participate in the democratic process. Whether you're Republican, Democrat, Independent, Green Party, or Purple Party, we all seem to respect folks who take the time to vote.

I feel both a sense of gratitude and responsibility when it comes to voting, and maybe it's heightened because I am a first-generation American. I believe we have a duty to thoughtfully discern and support people and policies that align with our values.

I saw how hard my parents worked when they were given the opportunity to immigrate to America. They worked at a small grocery store called Royal Pine Market in San Francisco's Nob-Loin neighborhood, eventually saving enough money to buy the business. From

7:00 in the morning to 11:00 in the evening, my mother, Sung Wha, worked tirelessly. My father, Tok, joined her after he returned home from a full day of work at a telecommunications company. On their only day off, Sunday, we went to church.

My brothers and I worked too, and oh, how we worked. We went to the store immediately after school ended and worked until the store's closing. As I think back on the life my kids have enjoyed, they had chores, but when I was a child, I had *work*. At the age of six, barely knowing English, I was delivering groceries in the neighborhood, bagging at the register, and sweeping floors. Our life revolved around the Royal Pine Market. For a time after our apartment burned down, we even lived above our grocery store, taking turns sleeping on an old mattress.

Though my parents were exhausted, they knew the opportunity afforded to them as Americans. They invested their lives, constantly working hard, for the sake of my two brothers and me, for the sake of our future. It's far from a perfect country, but to many, America remains a country of promise, a country of opportunity, where we can worship freely. I believe to whom much is given, much is expected, including civic engagement.

However, even if we're thoughtful, even if we are prayerful, even if we have the best of intentions to engage and carefully choose leaders at the ballot box, voting still has never been an equal-opportunity endeavor.

THE RIGHT (FOR SOME) TO VOTE

Imagine for a moment being turned away from a polling station because of your race or gender. This is not ancient history. It's part of the sometimes painful story of America.

The United States of America was founded in 1776. That's nearly 250 years ago, but African Americans only gained the right to vote 150 years ago with the passage of the Fifteenth Amendment. Let me adjust that statement. African American *men* gained the right to vote at that time (women of all races would still have to wait decades), and actually being able to vote is far different.

The hard reality was a variety of discriminatory practices kept many African Americans away from the voting booths. These obstacles included poll taxes, literacy tests, constitutional tests, and outright deception about the date and time of election days. These racist foils were most common in the South.

Then out of the hard-fought, Spirit-inspired Civil Rights Movement of the 1950s and 1960s came the 1965 Voting Rights Act, which eliminated those aforementioned barriers to vote.

The result of African Americans being able to vote was immediate:

> In 1965, at the time of the passage of the Voting Rights Act, there were six African-American members of the U.S. House of Representatives and no blacks in the U.S. Senate. By 1971, there were 13 members of the House and one black member of the Senate.[5]

As for women in America, they have only had the right to vote for the last one hundred years, and the long delay for equality was not for a lack of trying. The suffragist battle was led by women, who endured hostility and even beatings during their long quest. Outside the White House, they held signs, including one that read "Mr. President, how long must women wait for liberty?" Eventually, women, including the persistent and even-keeled Carrie Chapman Catt, persuaded President Woodrow Wilson to change his mind. In 1920, he signed the Nineteenth Amendment into law.[6] But in reality, the Nineteenth Amendment mostly enabled just white women to vote. For example, Native Americans didn't win the right to full citizenship until 1924 when President Calvin Coolidge signed the Indian Citizenship Act, also known as the Snyder Act. Because many states didn't want Native Americans to vote, they "were only able to win the right to vote by fighting for it state by state. The last state to fully guarantee voting rights for Native people was Utah in 1962."[7] So in essence, all Native American women throughout the country have only been able to vote since 1962.

It's a new time and everyone's able to vote now. Problem solved, right? I certainly wish that was true. To this day, not all is right in our union. Ethnic minorities, especially African Americans, still face significant burdens on the way to the ballot box.

For minority communities, even the act of voting continues to be a challenge. African Americans have historically had to spend much more time waiting to vote than white communities because of poor staffing at polling sites, with some voters waiting four hours or longer.

A Pew Charitable Research report found that in the 2016 election, African Americans waited sixteen minutes on average, Latinos waited thirteen minutes, and white people waited ten minutes. Wait times are improving overall, but disparities remain among the races.[8] I'm a fan of our all-mail elections here in Washington State, which has been shown to modestly improve voter turnout.[9] It also means I can vote while wearing my superfan BTS K-pop pajamas, my outfit of choice.

Even though we have constitutional amendments and laws to protect equality in our elections, the spirit behind those rules continues to be tested. And tested. And tested.

Hundreds of thousands of African Americans also lost their right to vote in places like Florida, because as felons, their voting rights have been stripped for life. In 2016, this impacted one in ten Floridians, and one in five African Americans in Florida.[10] The law has racist origins dating back to the end of the Civil War, when white politicians enacted a law to forbid felons from ever voting again, and then using postwar laws, they saddle black voters with criminal records, eliminating them from voting rolls.

The law's roots are so blatantly racist that one state leader later boasted that the postwar constitution would prevent Florida from being taken over by blacks, using a racial slur to describe them.[11]

But now, 65 percent of Floridians voted to overturn that law, opening the opportunity for 1.4 million people who have served their time to again vote, except those convicted of murder or a felony sexual offense. I am encouraged by this, and I'm also not surprised that the situation I've just described is being undermined as I write this book.

Why are we called to fair elections and to minister to those who have been convicted of crimes? Because we believe that those who are imprisoned are created in the image of God. Even if they are proven guilty, they are still made in the image of God.

Injustice is not a right and left issue. It's a right and wrong issue. Politics involves justice and injustice. The laws we pass affect people. As a pastor and believer, I am disturbed by what is happening in my country regarding voting and, realistically, what's been happening regarding voting *since the beginning of the country.*

For me, this all comes back to some core components of my faith. Honesty and loving my neighbor are two primary values that come to mind. It's safe to say that disenfranchising my neighbor's ability to vote would break both of those. If it's intentional disenfranchisement, it's wrong. If it's unintentional, careless disenfranchisement, it's still wrong.

To vote is to have a voice in our laws, a voice in our representation, a voice to select the future we desire. My family and I appreciate the opportunities we've enjoyed in this country, and I pray that those same opportunities—including the ability to vote—would someday be equally available to all.

ADVOCACY: A CALL FOR ALL

When I think about living out convictions in the political process, voting is clear. Political advocacy seems like a taller order. It may not be the first thing we think of. Even if we're not personally close to politicians or the political process, we see the vitriol and pressure on politicians to vote one way or another. We see the political machine.

Before I became involved in political advocacy, I thought it was something only experts should do. But through the years, after I've had the opportunity to meet with dozens of political leaders, I hear the same response, over and over: our voices matter. In short, advocacy matters. They tell me they listen to their constituents voicing their concerns. Though I am not an expert in all things, I strive to educate myself in order to be more informed and to better advocate for causes, issues, and vulnerable people.

An advocate is someone who pleads another's cause. It reminds me of the Spirit interceding on our behalf. The Spirit is our advocate, serving as our strength and our guide. In a sense, an advocate is a guide as well, when we help our elected leaders see the world with greater clarity.

Advocacy changes laws and systems that impact people. When we pursue justice for all through our advocacy, that's part of what it means to love our neighbors.

However, in my experience, churches and Christians rarely speak of advocacy. We hear and teach about compassion, grace, kindness, and generosity, which are beautiful and important. But I can't ever recall learning that advocacy matters—or even what advocacy was—as a younger Christian. And yet, woven throughout Scripture, I see the call to advocate and seek justice.

> Speak up for those who cannot speak for themselves,
>   for the rights of all who are destitute.
> Speak up and judge fairly;
>   defend the rights of the poor and needy.
>   (Prov. 31:8–9)

> Learn to do right; seek justice.
>   Defend the oppressed.
> Take up the cause of the fatherless;
>   plead the case of the widow. (Isa. 1:17)

> The King will reply, "Truly I tell you, whatever you did for one of the least of these brothers and sisters of mine, you did for me." (Matt. 25:40)

Speaking up for the world's poor through organizations such as the ONE campaign, World Relief, Bread for the World, and World Vision has been a recurring theme of my advocacy. The disparities in our world, even today, are shocking. More than one in ten people alive today do not have access to clean water. Without access to water, for example, women and girls walk six kilometers daily, lugging a forty-pound container, often through the dust and heat.

Women and girls collectively spend 200 million hours each day with this time-wasting, back-breaking work.[12] And it's not clean water either; it's dirty water that will make them sick, especially the smallest children. This affects every aspect of life, including school attendance and the percentage of kids who don't make it to their fifth birthday. Nearly 1,000 children under age five die every day from diarrhea caused by contaminated water, poor sanitation, and improper hygiene. The risk of a child dying before age five is around eight times higher in Africa than in Europe.[13]

But with advocacy and a political will to see something better, the tides are changing. Since 1990, 2.6 billion people have gained access to safe, clean water, according to the UN.[14] Just since 2008, the US government has helped more than 37 million of those people gain access.[15]

I've advocated publicly for this, talking with congressional leaders on Capitol Hill. With World Vision, I spoke in Washington, DC, for the Water for the World Act, a law to ensure that US funds for water, hygiene, and sanitation go to countries most in need, rather than countries in which the US has political interests. World Vision Advocacy offered me the facts and the connections to make the experience successful.

Beyond water, one of the most dramatic examples of political will is PEPFAR, the HIV and AIDS initiative started by then-president

George W. Bush to save and improve the lives of people living with HIV and AIDS. Right now, because of PEPFAR, 17 million men, women, and children are on lifesaving HIV treatment in Africa, and more than 2 million babies have been born HIV-free to HIV-positive mothers.[16] In just the first three years of the program, a Stanford University study estimated PEPFAR helped save more than 1 million lives.[17]

More than 1,000,000 lives!

Advocacy is part of loving your neighbor and an integral part of our discipleship. We are called to speak up for others, in the political system, in schools, in churches. We have voices, and we are expected to use them.

We need to demonstrate to the world God's love and concern for the poor, for the marginalized, for the widow, for the unborn, for those who don't have a voice. We need to be engaged in the process. My prayer to God is to have joy for the things that give Him joy, but for Him to break my heart for the things that break His.

Recently, as the work of advocacy gains more attention in Christian communities, it has been met with increased pushback and resistance. Some suggest that, as Christians, we should be about peace. Certainly, there's truth to this. As Christians, who doesn't like peace? As Christians, we should care deeply about peace, but all too often, our simple answer to the need for peace is "It's a sin issue" and, thus, we need a transformation of the heart. Yes, I agree: It's indeed a sin issue, and absolutely, Jesus is our great Reconciler and we must preach the good news that "Jesus saves!" But if we reduce sin merely to a personal issue, we neglect the reality of what happens when sin becomes communal and, as such, creates systems, institutions, and culture. Or to put it more simply, sinful people create sinful systems. Engaging both is essential if we're about the whole gospel and the kingdom of God.

In other words, there's a difference between peacemaking and peacekeeping. It's a subtle but dangerous mentality if our definition of peacemaking is really peacekeeping—as in, "Peace. Peace. Let's keep peace. Let's not rock the boat. It's working well for me."

This is why truth telling and advocacy are so critical in our discipleship and as part of our public witness in politics.

OUR THOUSANDS OF VOTES

Let's be informed by our convictions, as people of faith in Christ and with the kingdom of God in mind. Rather than being blinded by one issue, let's be informed on many issues and pray for convictions consistent with biblical foundations and a life ethic that encompasses the whole of life—from womb to tomb. And then vote.

We should obviously be open to supporting and voting for Christians. It matters. But it's not the only thing that matters. Remember that Christians are fallible humans who say and do some crazy stuff. There were Christian slave owners. There were Christians who supported Hitler. As a younger person, I felt it was particularly important to vote for Christians, and to this day, I am thrilled to vote for Christians, but that's not the sole litmus in order to get my vote.

Who are we voting for? What are we voting for? Do we vote simply to reduce the size of government because it's evil? Simply to increase the size of government because it's the answer to everything? Let's not be so simple minded. God made us to think complex thoughts, to exercise our judgment. He also gave us a road map of what to value and how to live, and that should impact the way we vote.

There's wisdom in how Lisa Sharon Harper conveys this value:

> First, we must recognize that we are not electing a Messiah. We will never have a perfect Presidential candidate. We're not trying to elect the person with a perfect policy platform. Second, we *must* ask the question *how would Jesus vote and who would Jesus vote for?* My criteria are outlined in Matthew 25. Jesus makes it clear in this text: These are the policies he cares about. He wants to make sure we understand that feeding the hungry, giving water to the thirsty, sheltering the homeless, are not side issues. They are central to our faith—even our salvation. Jesus says "I *am* the least of these."[18]

Although there will always be a winner and a loser after an election, it does matter how you play the game. Our character matters. Our integrity matters. Our witness matters. Exhibiting the fruit of the Spirit matters. It's not all about the outcomes of elections. We cannot be good with the mantra of "anything goes." That kind of mind-set will put us in the sewer with everyone else. We should squirm when we hear someone say, "It's just politics." We should repent if we are knowingly sharing falsehoods online. As Christians, we need to repent and then show a different way of doing it.

In our culture, we often talk about winning. We need to remember the way of Christ. Did Christ win in the end? Yes. But did He win in an earthly, political sense? No. He was executed between two criminals. I would call an execution a big X in the loss column if you're keeping that kind of score.

Jesus was not a winner by the world's standards. You could make a strong case that He was a loser. He had a big following for a while, but then people started to leave, and leave, and leave … and leave. His disciples left. One of his closest confidants betrayed Him. He was not wealthy; He was from Nazareth after all, and He did not have any property. He did not have an endorsement from powerful political groups. The religious leaders wanted Jesus to join their political machine, but He refused. People called Him demonic. And yet He stayed true to who He is, to the end.

What winner washes the feet of his subjects, knowing he was destined to die?

Jesus didn't play the game. He defied the game. We should too. His loss on earth was the biggest win ever for humanity. We are called to join Him, to exhibit a way of living and engaging that does not make sense by worldly definitions.

Much is made about the right to vote and the importance of election days. However, if we reduce civic engagement to a singular vote every two or four years, we are part of the problem. Yes, get out and vote. But don't just cast a vote. Embody your faith. Serve your neighbors. Advocate for the last and the least. Share the gospel. Work for the common good. Pursue justice. Seek the peace of your city.

Sometimes we get obsessed with the idea of changing the world. That can feel overwhelming. But changing the world doesn't mean you have to travel across oceans. Changing the world begins with our families and our neighborhoods. As Mother Teresa said, "Never worry about numbers. Help one person at a time and always start with the person nearest you."[19]

Let's embody our convictions every day with the very people around us. Every action we take is a vote for something. Little votes. Big votes. Actual votes. Votes of love. Votes of justice. Discipleship is every day, not just what we do on Sunday. We should be wary of those moments when we think we've won, as we've seen the power of losing it all.

As for me, you *will* see me at the voting booth next election day. At least in my voting pajamas.

Be informed.

Be prayerful.

Have integrity.

Vote your convictions.

And that's exactly what I'd like to share next—people embodying their convictions.

A BRAVE MAN

Voting is critically important, but we have many other ways to make our voice heard regarding things that matter. It's not only sharing articles on social media; it's by engaging the political process with the example of our lives.

Many of us are weary of the hatefulness that has come to define political dialogue and monologue in this country. Often those monologues come from media personalities, like Ann Coulter, who have created profitable personae.

In 2012, Coulter frequently targeted her political opponents, particularly President Obama, calling them by the outdated and vulgar

R-word that is offensive to so many, including actually mentally disabled people.[20]

In his very polite way, Frank Stephens wouldn't stand for it. He had spoken out before and written about the hurtful R-word and its repeated use in the so-called comedy *Tropic Thunder*.[21] He stood up to defend and represent others who, like him, had Down syndrome or were intellectually disabled in other ways. His open letter went viral after it was posted on the Special Olympics website.

"Come on Ms. Coulter, you aren't dumb and you aren't shallow. So why are you continually using a word like the R-word as an insult?" Stephens began. "I'm a 30-year-old man with Down syndrome who has struggled with the public's perception that an intellectual disability means that I am dumb and shallow. I am not either of those things, but I do process information more slowly than the rest of you. In fact, it has taken me all day to figure out how to respond to your use of the R-word last night."[22]

Coulter never apologized, by the way, but Stephens made lots of friends and fans.

Five years later, his friends list expanded again when actor Ashton Kutcher posted on Facebook Stephens' testimony before the House of Representatives Appropriations Subcommittee on Labor, Health and Human Services, and Education. It was shared more than a half million times. Although the pro-life movement seized the moment as being anti-abortion testimony, it actually was about funding for research to improve the lives of people with Down syndrome. Still, the value of a human life was clearly seen in the passion and warmth of Stephens. The line that captured headlines and hearts was simple and straightforward: "I am a man with Down syndrome and my life is worth living."

Stephens continued:

Why do I feel the need to make that point? Across the world, a notion is being sold that maybe we don't need to continue to do research concerning Down syndrome. Why? Because there are pre-natal screens that will identify Down syndrome in the womb, and we can just terminate those pregnancies. In places as wide-spread as Iceland, Denmark and South Korea, government officials have proclaimed that these government encouraged terminations will make them "Down syndrome free by 2030."

It is hard for me to sit here and say those words. Let's be clear, I completely understand that the people pushing that particular "final solution" are saying that people like me should not exist. They are saying that we have too little value to exist.

That view is deeply prejudiced by an outdated idea of life with Down syndrome. Seriously, I have a great life. I have been a guest lecturer at major universities. I have contributed to a best-selling book, had a feature role in an award-winning film, guest starred on an Emmy winning TV show, and spoken to thousands of young people about the value of inclusion in making America great. I've even been to the White House twice, and I didn't have to jump the fence either time.[23]

Stephens mentioned how common it has become to end pregnancies in abortion when Down syndrome is confirmed. In the United States, 67 to 85 percent of pregnancies of unborn children with Down syndrome are terminated.[24] It's higher in places like the UK, with 90 percent of pregnancies being aborted, and in the small country of Iceland, nearly 100 percent of the few pregnancies with Down syndrome detected are aborted.[25]

At Landspitali University Hospital in Iceland, where the majority of Icelandic children are born, Helga Sol Olafsdottir counsels women who are faced with a decision of whether or not to abort if Down syndrome is detected. She tells women they need to remember this is their life, and they have a right to choose what their life will look like. She dismisses the belief that some people call abortion murder.

"We look at it as a thing that we ended," Olafsdottir said. "We ended a possible life that may have had a huge complication … preventing suffering for the child and for the family."[26]

It's jarring to hear something like that and then listen to Stephens as he speaks before Congress.

Stephens is unfailingly polite and pleasant when he talks, whether before a congressional committee or in television interviews. He's engaging. He's confident. He says he's not looking for apologies; he just wants to change hearts. His letter to Coulter was signed, "A friend you haven't made yet."

FRED ROGERS

Fred Rogers' grandfather always told him he made him feel special just by being himself—a sentiment that was echoed throughout

Rogers' life in the gentle wisdom and stories he shared with millions of children.

As an insecure, overweight, and shy young man, Rogers was befriended by a football player at the high school he attended. When the athlete was injured and hospitalized, Rogers was asked to take notes for him in classes and to give him his homework. The two became friends, and when the football player returned to school with Rogers as his friend, others seemed to see a new side of him as well.[27] He became active in school activities, edited the school newspaper, and was president of his senior class. Confidence born of kindness was a message he shared repeatedly throughout his career.

Reared in a deeply religious home in Latrobe, Pennsylvania, Rogers planned to enter seminary and become a minister, but first he wanted a college degree. After a year at Dartmouth, he transferred to Rollins to study music, having loved and played the piano since childhood. He graduated and was only weeks from entering the seminary when he saw a television show for the first time. He was captivated by its potential but appalled by how poorly the new medium was being used.

Rogers decided to pursue television instead of seminary and went to work at NBC in New York, where he was floor manager for several shows. He soon concluded NBC wasn't interested in educational programming, so he moved to Pennsylvania and WQED, the first community television station in the United States.

Over the course of a few years, Rogers and the station's secretary, Josie Carey, created the program *The Children's Corner*. The show aired on a regional TV station with a $30 budget and was later picked up by other big markets, including as a Saturday-morning program on NBC called *Misterrogers* (one word). Rogers was the puppeteer, organ player, and writer. A chance for a daily show in Canada took him to Toronto for a year, but eventually he moved his young family back to Pittsburgh to be closer to relatives. There he finished a master of divinity degree and became ordained as a Presbyterian minister.

Mister Rogers' Neighborhood premiered in October of 1966 on WQED and in 1969 was picked up by PBS. That same year, Rogers went to Washington and testified before the US Senate Subcommittee on Communication. In less than seven minutes of unscripted comments, he spoke in the same slow, gentle tone that was his trademark and convinced senators to preserve $20 million in funding for PBS.

"We deal with such things as the inner drama of childhood. We don't have to bop someone over the head to make drama on the screen." He also talked about his concerns over gun violence on television—in 1969.[28] He explained that PBS offered a different kind of drama that children could relate to and learn from in stories about life in their families and their neighborhoods—and in *Mister Rogers' Neighborhood*.

"This is what I give, an expression of care every day to each child," Rogers told the Senate committee. "I end the program by saying, 'You've made this day a special day by just your being you. There's no person in the whole world like you and I like you just the way you are.'"

Indeed, Rogers never shied away from hard topics, including divorce, death, and war. At the height of racial tensions in the Civil Rights Movement, he invited the show's Officer Clemmons, an African American man, to sit next to him around a kiddie pool. Together they soaked their feet on a hot summer day. After the soak, Rogers helped Clemmons dry his feet with a towel. This "washing of the feet" happened just as Americans were learning about white people who were terrorizing black people in swimming pools by pouring bleach into the water.

On July 9, 2002, President George W. Bush awarded Rogers the Presidential Medal of Freedom for his service to the nation and contributions to children's education. By the time he died of stomach cancer on February 27, 2003, Rogers had earned forty honorary degrees, four Emmy Awards, and a Peabody Award. He was inducted into the Television Hall of Fame in 1999.[29]

That legacy is continued by the Fred Rogers Center, established in his honor to perpetuate three themes that were central to Rogers' life: helping children grow on the inside, helping them learn through relationships, and giving meaning to technology.[30]

And that he likes them, just the way they are.

EARLY-MORNING PRAYER MEETING FOR NORTH KOREA

While in seminary in my early twenties, I traveled to South Korea for what was initially intended to be a short summer internship. It evolved into a near two-year, full-time pastorate at a large and influential church in Seoul called Onnuri Church led by Rev. Yong Jo Hah. Looking back, my time at this church remains one of the most formative times of my life and leadership.

In one of the first conversations I had with Pastor Hah, he said, "Pastor Eugene, you are strongly encouraged to join the entire pastoral staff and some congregants for daily early-morning prayer meeting at 5:00 a.m."

"Wait, what? At what time? And was that a.m. or p.m.?" I asked.

Pastor Hah laughed at what he thought was a joke. He concluded the conversation with, "See you tomorrow morning."

The next morning, I forced my body to wake up at 4:30 a.m., and oh, it was so painful. Like a zombie in slow motion, I brushed my teeth, administered a quasi–face wash, put on the only suit I owned at the time, and barely made it to church by 4:59 a.m. I hurried into the sanctuary, wondering to myself, *Who's even going to even be here?*

I'll never forget the next scene. When I walked into the sanctuary to the pianist playing "Be Thou My Vision," about a thousand people rose to their feet and began to sing the first of several hymns and worship songs. Soon thereafter, Scripture was read and a short sermon was proclaimed. And then instructions were given to help guide prayer—but not just for their own lives, families, circumstances, and such. Those were certainly encouraged too, but I was moved by the exhortation to pray for the poor, the hungry, the oppressed, the last, lost, and least. Furthermore, there was a call to pray for the country, for government leaders, and then a fervent call to pray for the ongoing conflict between South Korea and North Korea. There was a call to pray for the unimaginable, for peace, unity, and reunification—not just of divided nations, but of thousands upon thousands of families. During this time, you could hear the wailing of tears.

The prayers for North Korea would be prayers I would hear (and join in prayer) every single morning. Every single morning. Honestly, some mornings I wondered and questioned if these prayers even mattered. The conflict between North and South Korea only seemed to be worsening. Technically, the war had never ended. While the Korean Armistice Agreement on July 27, 1953, had brought a halt to the horrible and brutal fighting that killed approximately 2.5 million, there was never a peace treaty. Ever since, there have been numerous outbursts and threats of conflict and tension.

Peace seemed unimaginable.

Unity seemed unattainable.

Reunification seemed impossible.

For these reasons, every single Korean (both in Korea and around the world) was stunned to witness the 2018 Donald Trump and Kim Jong-un summit and then on April 27, 2018, the signing of the Panmunjom Declaration between Kim and South Korea's president, Moon Jae-in.

As a Korean American, I've been asked by many people about my thoughts. While a peace treaty has yet to be signed, signaling an official end to the Korean War, what seemed impossible now seems possible. Certainly, it's important to recognize the initiative and leadership of the respective leaders above, but additionally, I always keep going back to the image of the hundreds of thousands of Korean Christians who gathered to pray for peace, unity, and reconciliation. Their prayers were not in vain. Our prayers are not in vain.

In our current cultural landscape, it often feels like the one who makes the most noise or proclaims the most outrageous accusations is most heard. This only seems to be increasing. We have to push back at these trends and remind ourselves and one another that kindness, civility, and meekness still matter. In fact, they've always mattered. Don't mistake humility with mediocrity or meekness with weakness. We don't have to be "jerks for Jesus" in order to stand out and influence others. May we remember who we are and, most importantly, *whom* we serve. May we pray, vote, raise our voices, march on the streets, and continue to pursue the hard, messy, and creative ways that can bring about change.

WHAT'S ON YOUR HEART AND MIND?

1. Read 1 Timothy 2:1–2. If praying for those in authority is your daily practice, how does it inform your political views?

2. If praying for those in authority isn't already your daily practice, how might you begin to incorporate it into your life?

3. As Christians, we commonly advocate for the rights of the unborn, as we should. What other people groups do you personally advocate for, and why?

CHAPTER 9

THOU SHALT LOVE GOD AND LOVE PEOPLE

The stereotypical abortion protestor is middle-aged, carries posters of fetuses (often dismembered or worse), and they shout. Really loud. These people aren't caricatures. They do exist. And they do shout. While they may have the best of intentions, protestors with graphic signs do more to set back the pro-life cause than help it in my opinion.

But it's erroneous to assume that all abortion protestors are mean spirited, cruel, and in-your-face. How do I know? Well, over the years, I've met some of them and even joined some of them outside clinics, in marches, or for prayer gatherings. One such person is Eleanor McCullen, who calls herself a sidewalk counselor. She greets women and men with a warm smile and says, "Good morning! Can I help you?"[1] I can attest that her smile and gentleness are as genuine and authentic as they come. It's clear, even in an initial conversation, that she loves Jesus and loves people.

For women heading into an abortion clinic, many overcome with shame, to hear a friendly, respectful voice is so disarming that they pay attention.

Eleanor looks like a grandma, and she is. She's in her seventies, plump, and has a glow about her. Eleanor invites women to her Boston home for chocolate-chip cookies. Or she drives them to a pregnancy-resource center not far away. She offers to have a baby shower, and she follows through. In the months and years that follow, Eleanor helps mothers get medical care, find jobs, or secure places to live. She pays to get refrigerators fixed, or pays a light bill, and she hosts spaghetti dinners and Christmas parties for the children.

Eleanor wasn't kidding when she asked women if she could help them.

Eleanor's refrigerator is covered with pictures of children who are not related to her, but who were once fetuses, in utero, headed with their mothers and sometimes their fathers or grandparents into a Boston abortion clinic. She estimates that about two hundred children are alive because she was able to show moms how much she genuinely cared.

Pro-choice advocates often say pro-lifers are just pro-birth, that if they were pro-life they would be equally active in helping women have what they need to raise a child—a job, healthcare, a home, emotional and financial support. That's fair criticism, but Eleanor McCullen actually does that. And there are so many more than the media or pro-life detractors would want to acknowledge.

When Massachusetts passed a law creating a thirty-five-foot buffer zone to keep protestors like her away from the entrance to abortion clinics, Eleanor immediately saw how it impacted her ability to gently, warmly connect with people. Eleanor sued for the right to be closer, and at the Supreme Court, she won.[2]

Eleanor never planned to become an activist. But for years now she's been showing up every Tuesday and Wednesday morning to pray and counsel, starting conversations as she prays.

A lifelong Catholic, Eleanor attributes her passion for this cause to the intervention of the Holy Spirit and a conversation with her priest. Her colleagues have called her Mother Teresa. Her husband, Joe, calls her a saint. And she's gotten him involved too, helping fathers with résumés, buying strollers and diapers and baby clothes. He doesn't go to the clinic with her, but he helps her support the mothers and fathers and babies who become children instead of statistics.

It's tough to imagine a moment with more political charge than when a pregnant woman walks into an abortion clinic. And yet Eleanor has been able to make hundreds of friends in that moment, among the many others who dismiss her.

Women believe Eleanor loves them, because she does, just as Jesus has loved her. More than one baby girl has been named Eleanor after the mother heard a friendly "Good morning!" that changed her mind, her life, and the life of her child.

May we all have the Spirit move within us like He has moved in Eleanor. May our passion and convictions in politics never supersede our love for God and neighbor—including neighbors who don't share our politics.

FINDING FAMILY

Perhaps you're not a congressperson (only 535 Americans are), but you want to live out your convictions. Do not fear, you have many opportunities; it's simply a matter of connecting with the one that resonates with you. For retirees Doug and Lisee McGlashan of Seattle, two of their most notable convictions are young men from Ghana—Kwaku and Arafat. These young men have chosen to call Doug and Lisee not ma'am and sir, but mom and dad.

Doug was looking for a way to serve others, so he signed up to be a cultural companion with World Relief, a Christian humanitarian organization. Part of World Relief's work is centered in the US, helping to resettle refugees in America who have left their country in a time of crisis. Kwaku and Arafat feared for their lives for different reasons and left their home country, seeking political asylum.

After refugees go through extensive background checks, the US government works through organizations like World Relief to place them in a community and, in many cases, teach them basic life skills. That's where cultural companions come in. They show new folks the ropes, because even flipping on and off the lights can be a new experience for some.

Doug and Lisee have gone much further than teaching Kwaku and Arafat survival skills. When Doug met Arafat, he quickly moved beyond the formalities and began answering questions about cars, as Arafat was planning to buy one. Then they talked about education. Then about American football. Then about qualities to look for in a partner. Arafat had not only found a cultural companion; he'd found a dad.

From Liz Hadley at World Relief Seattle:

Arafat grew to know Lisee as well and naturally referred to her as "mom." When I met with the family over pizza to hear their story, Arafat explains to me that he lost both his parents when he was young. He grew quiet and, in a manner fitting of a toast, described how much respect he had for Doug and Lisee, how much they had helped him, welcomed him and loved him. Turning to look at Doug and Lisee, Arafat said "I love you dad, I love you mom." It was all I could do to not drown my slice of pizza in tears.

On the kitchen counter when you walk into the McGlashan house, sits a little shrine capturing their family: a photo of their adult daughter, a picture of their two Goldens, and a small balloon that says "I love you mom." Lisee explains to me that this gift is from her boys. For Mother's Day this past year, Arafat brought over flowers, a massive teddy bear, and this balloon. The balloon now sits amongst the mementos to biological children and pets they've cared for over years. It's clear that the concept of family is being blown wide open for the McGlashans.[3]

In time, Arafat introduced the McGlashans to Kwaku and then many more friends from their ad hoc community of other "boys," refugees who have resettled in Seattle. The McGlashans are amazed at the lengths these young men went to in order to come to America, circuitous routes that involved detentions, bus rides, kindhearted strangers, and setbacks. Doug and Lisee hear these stories around their dinner table when they invite the boys over. Young men seeking safety found a family as well.

THE MOST POWERFUL SERMON

In 2017, I traveled to Lebanon for some refugee-related advocacy and work. While there, I was hosted by the local leaders of World Vision. We visited several sites that One Day's Wages had helped fund with resources, including refugee camps in various spaces—big refugee camps in the middle of nowhere, urban spaces, and even some churches.

I will never forget a meeting I had with a local Lebanese pastor. For security purposes, we were asked not to share the name of the pastor, the church, or the location, so I'll refer to him as Pastor Maheer.

Pastor Maheer led a church near the border between Lebanon and Syria. Because of war and conflict, Syria has had a massive refugee crisis since 2011 that has tragically created approximately 5.3 million registered Syrian refugees in neighboring countries and 6.2 million internally displaced persons.[4] The United Nations High Commissioner for Refugees (UNHCR) estimates that Lebanon alone hosts approximately 1 million registered Syrian refugees.[5] Nongovernment organization (NGO) leaders on the ground actually believe it's closer to 1.5 million refugees if you also include nonregistered refugees. Of this number, 74 percent lack legal status.[6] As a result, it has caused significant issues in Lebanon. Even before the refugee crisis, unpredictable tension between Lebanon and Syria existed ever since Syria's occupation of Lebanon in the 1980s.

This Lebanese pastor was leading a "large and successful" church made up of nearly all Lebanese congregants. But once as he was praying for the vision of the church, he sensed the Holy Spirit convicting him to do the unimaginable—to open his church and welcome Syrian refugees. To care and love them. To house and feed them. To love like Jesus.

Pastor Maheer shared vulnerably how, at first, he struggled with this conviction and kept praying, "Jesus, am I hearing this correctly?"

Finally, with much reservation and fear, he shared this vision with his congregation, and it didn't go well. His congregants were furious about the audacity he had to propose the idea of inviting those Syrian refugees—nearly all Muslims—to their church. More than pushback, he began to receive threats from both his church and the larger community. Eventually, some folks decided to leave the church. While he didn't share the specific number, the local NGO working with their church shared that 90 percent of the congregation left the church.

90 percent. Let that sink in. It's not quite a formula for church growth.

But Pastor Maheer felt he needed to obey the Holy Spirit and did his best to not only open the church to house refugees but to welcome and love them. Then, something amazing happened. Some of the Syrian Muslim refugees began to inquire about the church's beliefs, about their faith in Jesus. Soon, some of them started coming to worship gatherings. Soon, some of them made decisions to follow Jesus. Soon, some of them were baptized. And the next thing you know, not only did the church regain the 90 percent of the congregation that left, but it began to grow beyond. Some of those who had left decided to return. And for the refugees who didn't inquire about Jesus, visit the church services, or become Christians? Pastor Maheer kept obeying the Holy Spirit to welcome and love them. Sometimes, the most powerful sermon we can preach is the one we embody.

Thank you, Pastor Maheer. We need more examples like this in our lives. We need more of this kind of love in our churches.

During this intense political landscape, we can have our views and convictions. And it's likely that we may not agree on every single aspect. But how are we living out our faith in Jesus? How are we sharing the love and grace of our Lord Jesus Christ?

A RECOMMITMENT TO THE WHOLE GOSPEL

The gospel simply means "good news." And what is this good news?

God created the universe. Because of sin and rebellion, humanity was separated from God, but the good news is that God did not give up on His creation. For God so loved the world that He sent His only begotten Son, Jesus Christ.[7]

The good news is Jesus came for sinners. This includes you and me. This includes people of all various political inclinations. Jesus rescues sinners. Jesus saves desperate and depraved sinners like you and me. And Jesus offers us the gift of life and salvation for those who place their trust in Him.

This is truly good news. May we not wane in our passion in declaring this good news with the whole world.

However, it's important for us to speak of the whole gospel. If we're not careful, and especially in a very consumer-oriented society, this can give birth to a skewed, narcissistic, self-centered theology that's exclusively about me, myself, and I.

My personal relationship with Jesus.

My quiet time.

My church.

My small group.

My family.

My marriage.

Me, myself, and I spirituality.

While it's true that Jesus loves you, He doesn't love only you. This is why the greatest commandments are for us to love God and to love our neighbors.

To only convey a personal gospel that revolves around an individual is a limited gospel, a partial gospel, and even a false gospel. The good news is that God is still at work to redeem, restore, and reconcile. While it's clear that the world is deeply broken and fallen, the story is not yet finished. God is not yet done. As such, the whole gospel declares that God cares about collective human flourishing. This is, after all, His creation. In other words, the world matters. Justice and reconciliation are not tertiary issues. They matter to God. Refugees matter. Migrant and immigrant children and families in holding and detention centers matter. Poor people matter. The oppressed matter. The unborn matter. Indeed, God cares for all of His creation!

REMEMBER, JESUS LOVES PEOPLE

Yes, Jesus flipped tables and used some intense language to call out religious leaders. The temptation in our culture is to corner Jesus into one side or isolate one verse, or one scene, or one interaction, and then imagine He was only about one thing. If we're honest, it may be because we want to be justified in our actions and there's nothing like trying to mold Jesus into our image or our corner. We want Jesus to be about ourselves.

When I reflect on Jesus' actions in the temple as he flipped tables and chased away money changers, I don't see incivility; I see both courage and righteous anger. When I reflect on Jesus calling out religious leaders as a brood of vipers, hypocrites, blind guides, serpents, and fools, I see a shepherd who loves His flock and who's unafraid to challenge the status quo and hold leaders accountable for their lack of compassion and their hypocrisy.

But Jesus wasn't known only for overturning tables, speaking prophetically, and challenging hypocritical leaders. He cared for the lost, the last, and the least. Story after story, parable after parable, interaction after interaction, meeting after meeting, we witness a Jesus who shows us who God is, because He is God incarnate. We see the kingdom of God both preached and embodied through Jesus.

Even the disciples themselves were a hodgepodge, an eclectic mixture of people who had different professions, backgrounds, convictions, family histories, genealogies, and political views.

AN ECLECTIC MIX

Over the centuries, a myth has emerged that Jesus called a group of twelve simple, uneducated guys who were mostly alike except for the one who was a traitor. The reality is different. The apostles were unique individuals. Jesus called people into His ministry who would challenge one another and represent the fact that this new kingdom is for all.

Peter and Andrew were brothers and fishermen. Andrew had also been a disciple of John the Baptist, so perhaps he was connected to the Essenes or a similar group.

Bartholomew, also called Nathaniel, is thought by some to have been of royal blood, at least a little. His name means "Son of Talmai."[8] Talmai was king of Geshur whose daughter, Maacah, was the wife of David, mother of Absalom.

James (the elder) and John were brothers and fishermen.

James (the younger) and Jude (also called Thaddeus) were brothers too. Jude was also called a zealot.

Simon was a zealot too.

Matthew was a tax collector. Tax collectors had a bad reputation for stealing from people and being too cozy with the Romans. They definitely didn't hang out with zealots who wanted to destroy the government.

Phillip was probably another fisherman, and Thomas probably wasn't.

Judas Iscariot, the traitor, was also the treasurer, and his politics are a bit uncertain. Many have speculated he betrayed Jesus out of political motives, hoping to spur an uprising.

The point is that the first disciples of Jesus were an eclectic mixture of people from various backgrounds, stories, genealogies, and even political inclinations—and yet, Jesus chose them.

Jesus welcomed each of them to His kingdom work; and even while the disciples stumbled and bumbled along, they learned to submit their lives to the lordship of Christ. And this is what discipleship is about: to surrender our lives to Christ. To yield our swords and our words to Christ; to relinquish our pride and surrender our hearts to Christ; to surrender our thoughts to Christ; to yield our loyalties to gods, kings, mammon, tribes, nationalism, and other earthly identities to the lordship of Christ.

Is it difficult? Yes.

Is it messy? Yes.

Is it confusing? At times, yes.

Discipleship is not for the faint of heart.

But Jesus has room and space for everyone, even those with different views, affiliations, leanings, and loyalties. There are many stories of His scandalous love, mercy, and grace. One of the most scandalous involves a tax collector by the name of Zacchaeus. Granted, Matthew the disciple was a tax collector too, but I suspect that when Jesus engaged in a conversation with Zacchaeus and then invited Himself to his home, everyone lost their minds. Zacchaeus was considered a chief tax collector, which basically meant that he worked for the villainous Roman Empire, the oppressors of the Jewish people. Zacchaeus not only swindled people for a living, but he also worked for the other side, the evil side, the nasty side, the oppressive side. It's for these reasons that the Jewish people universally despised all tax collectors. They were utterly vilified. How much?

Matthew, Mark, and Luke all believed it was important to accentuate how scandalous it was for Jesus to eat with such men like Zacchaeus and other tax collectors.

Then Levi held a great banquet for Jesus at his house, and a large crowd of tax collectors and others ate with them. And the Pharisees and the teachers of the law who belonged to their sect complained to His disciples, "Why do you eat and drink with tax collectors and sinners?"[9]

Jesus was well aware of His dinner guests, yet He still sat at the table and ate. In the hours before His capture, He ate with the one who would betray Him. In modern culture, we are comfortable with cutting people out, but Jesus showed radical inclusion.

THE SCANDALOUS LOVE OF JESUS

Zacchaeus probably had few friends, and they were most likely fellow tax collectors. He was a person of privilege and wealth yet was poor in spirit, truly hated, vilified, and demonized. When he heard Jesus was in town, Zacchaeus climbed up a sycamore tree to get a better view. Short-person problems, so I relate. Then something extraordinary happened that gave us another glimpse of the countercultural, radical nature of Jesus and the kingdom of God.

Jesus saw Zacchaeus, which is especially meaningful because many either ignored Zacchaeus or had choice words for him.

He then spoke to Zacchaeus. With kindness and respect. With civility. With love. And straight to the point, Jesus invited Himself over. "Hurry and come down, for today I must stay at your house."[10] Jesus had been the guest of notorious sinners, self-righteous Pharisees, and faithful supporters, but only here do we read of Him initiating an invitation.

God calls all people, even men like Zacchaeus, unto Himself. He meets us where we are and pursues us so that in our discipleship, we surrender ourselves to Him more and more. May we understand His radical love for us so we can extend this love for others. Jesus loves not only you but also those who disagree with you. If you're a flaming liberal, He loves the conservative. If you're a die-hard conservative, He loves the liberal. He loves people from the elite coast and the rural towns. He loves Republicans, Democrats, and even those noncommittal Independents. He loves immigrants and refugees—wherever they may be from. And while I know that many will be up in arms,

Jesus has no use for guns, but He loves those members of the NRA. (Get it?)

Want more crazy talk? He loves white supremacists. I know this is insane and nonsensical. Jesus is absolutely and unequivocally against the sin of white supremacy and violence. Jesus is against the sin of racism, xenophobia, and misogyny, and as such, Christians must be against the things that Jesus would be against. We must name sin for what it is, invite folks living in sin to repentance, demand that people stop wreaking violence and havoc on others and repent. We must pray for changed hearts and also work to change unjust and broken systems and structures.

To declare that Jesus loves people isn't permission to be soft and passive on sin. We can condemn injustice. We can and must condemn racism, xenophobia, and misogyny. We must condemn violence. We must condemn white supremacy. We must condemn the exploitation of children and women. Whatever one's views, we must condemn when there's violence inflicted against the LGBTQ community. To declare that Jesus loves people is not at odds with pursuing justice.

We can be against sin, broken systems, and certain policies and still remember that God loves the individuals involved. I have a strong reaction to Ann Coulter and Cecile Richards, the former president of Planned Parenthood. I condemn Ann's rhetoric and condemn Cecile's championing of abortion, but in my self-righteousness, I must remind myself that Jesus loves them. Yes, we can be against policies, someone's politics and actions … and still acknowledge their humanity and Jesus' love for them.

Of course, we pursue God's kingdom, and there are times when it is necessary to march, protest, fight, protect, or push back—but we can't forget that His love is radical. If we ever believe that someone is outside of God's redemptive love and grace, we need to reexamine our theology of God's love and grace.

Speaking of white supremacists …

BEFRIENDING HATE WITH LOVE

Daryl Davis said, "If you spend five minutes with your worst enemy—it doesn't have to be about race, it could be about anything … you will find that you both have something in common. As you build upon those commonalities, you're forming a relationship and as you build that relationship, you're forming a friendship."[11]

Davis, a black man and professional blues musician, was talking about Klansmen. *A black man forming friendships with Klansmen.* That's not a typo.

For more than twenty years, he's been getting acquainted with card-carrying members of the Ku Klux Klan, finding something in common, and collecting robes in the process—a lot of white-hooded robes. He told NPR he has about two hundred. He told the *Washington Post* he has about fifty.[12] Either way, that's a lot of white sheets for a black man who spends his nights and weekends playing piano.

The piano playing is what got it started, actually. He was the only black member of his band and, often, the only black man in the bar where they played. It was at one of these gigs that a white man struck up a conversation with him about the music, saying he'd never heard a black man play like Jerry Lee Lewis. The casual conversation became a bit of a boogie-woogie history lesson, then the white man told Davis he had never shared a drink with a black man.

A confused Davis wondered how that was possible, especially given that his bar companion was older than he was. Eventually, the white man's friend prodded him to reveal to Davis that he was a member of the KKK. Davis laughed, not believing him. Then the white man pulled out his wallet and showed his Klan identification card. Davis stopped laughing but didn't resort to violence or run. Instead, it was the beginning of a real relationship. A couple of years later the man left the Klan and gave his robes to Davis.

A lot of black activists are critical of Davis' approach. They think he's naive, that he doesn't share the experience of many black Americans. He doesn't dispute that part. He grew up the son of a Foreign Service employee, attending international schools he's likened to little United Nations, while other black children stateside were still in largely segregated schools. But he stands by his methods.

It's a radical approach to open yourself up and befriend those who hate you, and you can't get much more radical than a black man caring about a Klansman. As you can expect, this unconventional way of love doesn't always work, if you consider success in strictly temporal, earthly terms. It's the way of Christ, though. Just as Jesus tells us to love God and love our neighbors, the Spirit moves when we take that step to love the unlovable, to show them the humanity that they've attempted to deny us. It is through actions like these that we can see Christ's holy reconciliation in our relationships and our world.

WHAT'S ON YOUR HEART AND MIND?

1. Have you ever attempted to befriend someone who persecuted you (or your race, gender, etc.)? What was the end result?

2. What does loving God look like in your life?

3. Read Luke 6:32–36. What does loving your neighbor look like in your life? What are some of the ways you show love to your neighbor?

CHAPTER 10

THOU SHALT BELIEVE JESUS REMAINS KING

Whenever I speak about God's sovereignty, I'm met with responses and criticisms such as, "Eugene, this shows your privilege."

Rather than get defensive, I own it. I don't need to banter with the privilege police. I acknowledge that I'm privileged. While I have my own stories of trials, prejudice, hunger, struggling to make ends meet, a season living in our family's grocery store as a child, surfing couches with my family as an adult while trying to make ends meet ... I know I am still privileged. But it doesn't take away from my conviction that God remains in control. It's the foundation on which we started this book and constantly remind ourselves through the chaos and craziness of our society and culture.

Yet, placing trust in God's sovereignty is not permission and license to disengage from the chaos and craziness. If anything, it gives us grounding, fortitude, and perseverance. For example, as I said before, I'm not suggesting that elections, politics, and government aren't important.

They are! Remember, politics matter because politics impact policies that affect people. The policies of our government have tremendous significance, especially to the marginalized. Tim Keller, founding pastor of Redeemer Presbyterian Church in New York City, articulated the danger of isolating our faith to simply "preach the gospel":

> We must not think it really possible to transcend politics and simply preach the gospel. Those Christians who try to avoid all political discussions and engagement are essentially casting a vote for the social status quo. Since no human society reflects God's justice and righteousness perfectly, supposedly apolitical Christians are supporting many things that displease God. So to not be political is to be political. Churches in the U.S. in the early nineteenth century that did not speak out about slavery because that would have been "getting political" were actually supporting the slavery status quo by staying silent.[1]

Until this world is done and the next has come, we are all impacted by politics in some shape or another. If you're not impacted by politics, your neighbor may be. If not your literal neighbor, then your neighbor on the other side of town, or your neighbor in an inner city or rural town, or perhaps, your neighbor in another country. The Bible is clear about the command to love our neighbors, and Jesus went to great lengths to show what that looks like.

We must all be aware of the impact of political decisions and engage in constructive discourse and action involving our governance. God deeply cares about our neighbors, and He expects us to care as well. What happens in the world, our nation, and our communities happens to people, and those people are our neighbors. In fact, the world's population is approximately 7.7 billion people, and each is an image bearer of God.

GOD IS AT WORK

It's true, the world is broken, but the story of redemption is not yet finished. Jesus came during the darkest hour, bringing hope and light. Even in times of apparent silence, God is not absent. God is at work. God is not yet done.

Though earthly leaders may have the power to mistreat, marginalize, and persecute, and though their policies or inaction may even harm or kill people, we follow a leader who remains true and just.

Though our earthly leaders may take the side of the powerful and greedy at times, we follow a leader whose heart aches for the broken, destitute, and poor in spirit.

Earthly leaders may act in ways that are morally bankrupt and cruel. Leaders from every political stripe can be drawn to power as a self-aggrandizing, egocentric, narcissistic exercise. They may even hear the cries of their people and ignore them or vilify them.

But our Triune God—the one, true leader of all—will always be on the right side of history. He will always stand for justice, righteousness, and compassion. He will always have the last word. Our Creator moves in the world in ways that would differ from how you or I might behave if we had His authority and power. Thank God for that.

His inspired timing and judgment are His own, not ours, and thank God for that.

Our King is righteous and all-knowing. He rules over all eternity, regardless of who in earthly authority rules the land for a moment of time.

Our King knows us, and still loves us.

Our King knows us, and still sacrificed all for us.

Our King knows us, and still invites us to be in relationship with Him. He invites us to live in His kingdom, where He will be in power and authority forever and ever.

We have citizenship in a much better place, and our time as citizens in this place begins today. He says we are needed in this kingdom, to live the lives He calls us to live. As citizens of His kingdom, He expects us to act, to be His hands and feet while here on earth. To live out Micah 6:8, to act justly, love mercy, and walk humbly with our God.

As Christ followers, we are expected to live differently, for we are set apart.

> But you are a chosen people, a royal priesthood, a holy nation, God's special possession, that you may declare the praises of him who called you out of darkness into his wonderful light. Once you were not a people, but now you are the people of God; once you had not received mercy, but now you have received mercy. (1 Pet. 2:9–10)

We are invited into God's holy work. He trusts us to be His people, and to love others in His name, though we are fallible and at times we are scared.

Things are done differently in this kingdom, and that is very good news indeed.

GOVERNMENT IS NOT A FOUR-LETTER WORD

If we are called to build God's kingdom, what should the role of politics be in our lives as Christians?

As you may agree, government can be frustrating. If you don't agree, go get your driver's license renewed. I'll wait. Government is frustrating because humans are involved, and humans are fallible … and can be both life-giving and frustrating.

It reminds me of the dynamics within any church. Your church, my church, any church. The best things about church are the people. The most difficult things about church are the people, and often, it's the same people. Shh, don't tell my church folks I said that.

But without people, we wouldn't have order emerge from chaos. Without people, we would not have care for the needy, a wise word for the searching, or songs for those in spiritually dry seasons of life. People are what society is all about.

When we talk about the fabric of society, we are usually referring to the order created by three social institutions, with people at the core. I believe these are God inspired, though imperfect. These social institutions are key for human flourishing. Without them, our social order would not function as we see it today.

The institutions are family, government, and the church. Some scholars define more than three, but these three are primary. The challenge for us today is that we are living in a time of anti-institutionalism. We see traditional family life and family commitment in a place of flux, traditional church being rejected, and government as we have known it becoming more unpopular than ever. We have those who believe government is the answer to every societal ill, and those who believe government by its very nature intrudes on our God-given freedoms.

In order to ensure that the people maintain these rights, government has its role. In the Federalist Papers, founding father James Madison wrote his defense of the new constitution and new government:

> If men were angels, no government would be necessary. If angels were to govern men, neither external nor internal controls on government would be necessary. In framing a government which is to be administered by men over men, the great difficulty lies in this: you must first enable the government to control the governed; and in the next place oblige it to control itself. A dependence on the people is, no doubt, the primary control on the government; but experience has taught mankind the necessity of auxiliary precautions.[2]

In 1959, 171 years after President Madison wrote the above letter, Rev. Dr. Martin Luther King Jr. addressed the Religious Leaders Conference in Washington, DC, at Vice President Richard Nixon's request. The topic: how religious leaders might support Nixon's program to eliminate discrimination in employment in government contracts.

King challenged religious leaders to do far better, because of their faith. He said:

Any religion that professes to be concerned with the souls of men and is not concerned with the slums that damn them, the economic conditions that strangle them, and the social conditions that cripple them, is a spiritually moribund religion in need of new blood.[3]

We need courageous leaders who are willing to wisely navigate complexity in a divisive world. Consider the incredible story of Nelson Mandela, the former president of South Africa. Beginning in 1964, Mandela labored virtually every day for thirteen years as a prisoner for his convictions. In total, he spent eighteen years in Robben Island, the isolated prison located approximately five miles offshore from Cape Town. I'll never forget pacing back and forth in his seven-by-nine-foot jail cell during my visit to the island in 2007. Sitting, pacing, pondering, reflecting, praying, and imagining his circumstances, doubts, fortitude, and tenacity.

It's impossible to read about the life of Mandela and not draw at least a few parallels between his transformational journey and that of the apostle Paul. Violence. Passion. Imprisonment. Redemption. They even both have jailer stories. Paul's jailer was spared from his own hand when Paul and the others told him not to harm himself. Despite an earthquake that loosened the prisoners' chains, they all remained there; he needed not fear his Roman superiors.[4]

Mandela, after twenty-seven years of imprisonment (split between Robben Island, Pollsmoor Prison, and Victor Verster Prison) and four years of freedom, became the first black president of his beloved South Africa and invited his white jailer to his inauguration.[5] It must have felt like an earthquake. But Mandela's life and leadership are not without critics. Some saw him as too willing to compromise, too eager for reconciliation, too slow to address the AIDS crisis. But a world watched him transform a nation and its people in undeniable ways.

In 2015, the World Economic Forum cited major changes in South Africa[6] after Mandela's release from Victor Verster Prison on February 11, 1990, which continued during his presidency (1994–1999). Personal incomes increased and inflation dropped. Unemployment, which remains high even today, improved in the years after his release and under his leadership. Lifting of sanctions by the international community brought about dramatic increases in trade.

Historians and biographers have debated Mandela's religious affiliation, but his own words suggest a thoughtful understanding of a Messiah who saves. In his address to the Zionist Christian Church's Easter Conference in 1994 he said:

> The Good News borne by our risen Messiah who chose not one race, who chose not one country, who chose not one language, who chose not one tribe, who chose all of humankind!
>
> Each Easter marks the rebirth of our faith. It marks the victory of our risen Saviour over the torture of the cross and the grave.
>
> Our Messiah, who came to us in the form of a mortal man, but who by his suffering and crucifixion attained immortality.
>
> Our Messiah, born like an outcast in a stable, and executed like [a] criminal on the cross.

Our Messiah, whose life bears testimony to the truth that there is no shame in poverty: Those who should be ashamed are they who impoverish others.

Whose life testifies to the truth that there is no shame in being persecuted: Those who should be ashamed are they who persecute others.

Whose life proclaims the truth that there is no shame in being conquered: Those who should be ashamed are they who conquer others.

Whose life testifies to the truth that there is no shame in being dispossessed: Those who should be ashamed are they who dispossess others.

Whose life testifies to the truth that there is no shame in being oppressed: Those who should be ashamed are they who oppress others.[7]

Mandela led with humility and wisdom, seeing potential in the unwritten future of his country. He was one of many individuals through whom we can see glimmers of the kingdom. But only through one man are we able to see the kingdom in its fullness.

AN UPSIDE-DOWN KINGDOM

A man rode a donkey down a rocky hill toward a village, hearing shouts of adulation as he entered the community. He knew this was the time to show the world with more clarity who He really was, the King who came to deliver us. Behind Jesus and His borrowed donkey was dust in the air from the journey, and ahead was a celebration, and the fulfill-ment of an ancient prophecy.

Zechariah had prophesied this event some four hundred years earlier:

> Rejoice greatly, O daughter of Zion; shout, O daughter of Jerusalem: behold, thy King cometh unto thee: he is just, and having salvation; lowly, and riding upon an ass, and upon a colt the foal of an ass. (Zech. 9:9 KJV)

"Hosanna, hosanna in the highest!" shouted his disciples. "Blessed is the king who comes in the name of the Lord!"

On the ground below Jesus and the donkey were the cloaks of his admirers and branches from trees spread across the road, thrown down as a welcome mat—an act of royal homage.

The crowds that went ahead of him, and those that followed con-tinued their praise.

"Hosanna in the highest heaven!"[8]

It was a moment to celebrate the miracles of God, and an unlikely entrance for a King. It happened in a small village. A humble King. A borrowed donkey, along with its foal. It all seems upside down for a King. Then, when He entered Jerusalem, the whole city was stirred.

Who was this man?

Who was this supposed King, this prophet from Nazareth in Galilee?

Let's just say what many were probably thinking: *He's a king? He's from an obscure town. Can anything good come from Nazareth?*[9] A humble King. Those words together may seem like an oxymoron, both in the time of Jesus and even in our world today, two thousand years later. Jesus is a King who not only taught us to turn the other cheek, but who willingly died on our behalf.

His apostles lived this out as well. The apostle Paul called Christians to seek to live in peace. And yet he said this in a context in which it was dangerous to be a follower of Jesus. Christ was crucified, and nearly all His closest disciples were killed because of their faith. John the Baptist, Jesus' cousin, was beheaded.[10] James was put to death by the sword.[11] Paul was also beheaded, by Emperor Nero.[12]

I could choose many examples to show the nature of Christ, but there is one poignant moment that illuminates the countercultural nature of Jesus: His triumphal entry into Jerusalem. One could call it an ancient and holy presidential motorcade.

LIMOUSINES, PRIVATE JETS, AND POWER

When I think about Jesus the King's limo in this story, a donkey, I am struck by His countercultural choice of transportation. To put it simply, the King of Kings was not rolling in a Cadillac Escalade with 24-inch rims. It was not a horse, the caddy of the day. Jesus had a dusty journey on the back of an ass.

Throughout the Bible, we find the donkey is an animal symbolic of humility, peace, and also of Davidic royalty.[13] Donkeys are not flashy. They serve behind the scenes and help where they are needed. Even to this day, donkeys are considered reliable helpers. During Jesus' time, they were a symbol of industry, peace, and at times, wealth. Meanwhile, horses were a sign of not only wealth but also war, power, and the strength of military force.

The way a ruler would enter a city could tell you a lot about him and his status. For example, the famous Greek author Plutarch described how the Roman general Aemilius Paulus made his entrance into the city of Rome after a crushing victory over the Macedonians. (Spoiler: it was not on a donkey.)

> When Aemilius entered Rome, Plutarch tells us, his triumphant procession through the city lasted no less than three days. The first day was dedicated to carrying around Rome all the artwork that Aemilius and his army had looted from Macedonia. The second day they displayed all the weapons of the Macedonians. When the day finally came for Aemilius himself to make his glorious entrance he was preceded by 250 oxen, whose horns were covered in gold. Afterwards came the vessels carrying the gold coins that had been taken, according to Plutarch no less than 7,700 kg or 17,000 pounds. Following all the plunder, Aemilius had the king of Macedonia and his extended family parade through the city of Rome, having to endure the shame of their complete defeat by the Roman general. With such a demonstration of his power and might, Aemilius himself entered Rome, mounted on a chariot with glorious adornments. He wore a purple robe, interwoven with gold, and he carried his laurels in his right hand. Accompanying him, he had a whole choir, who would sing hymns, praising the military victories of the great Aemilius.[14]

Meanwhile, modern-day leaders show they as well want to visibly display power, especially those whose rule can be defined as militaristic or authoritarian. Kim Jong-un, the brutal dictator of North Korea, follows in the footsteps of his father and grandfather, believing he must show military might in the most grandiose way possible. Kim demands parades through Pyongyang with tanks and missiles, with thousands of soldiers in uniform marching in formation.[15] One of his favorite modes of transport is a bulletproof train stocked with wine and cheese.[16] On several occasions, the North Korean press service has released carefully composed propaganda photos of Kim studiously watching test launches of intercontinental ballistic missiles, binoculars in hand.[17] And beyond just photos, he has threatened to lob missiles at America.[18]

For Russian president Vladimir Putin, riding shirtless on a horse is his glamour shot of choice,[19] as he projects his image of power and masculinity. Beyond his distinctly equestrian fashion choice, Putin also makes clear by his actions that he is willing to invade his weaker neighbors, including Crimea.[20]

Even in the United States, our president serves as commander in chief, the ultimate authority over the military. America is a land, not a military rule, but one with leadership steeped in powerful imagery. Regardless of who the president is, we expect he or she will be portrayed with strength. Air Force One. Marine One. Armored limos. Surprise visits with troops stationed in war zones. Red or blue, our recent presidents wear bomber jackets with the presidential seal.

Power. Prowess. Military might.

Psalm 20:7 cuts to the heart of the matter: "Some boast in chariots and some in horses, but we will boast in the name of the LORD, our God."[21]

Indeed. It makes such sense, then, that the King of Kings and Lord of Lords chose a donkey for His grand entrance. Jesus rode in on an ass at His own inauguration. Goodness gracious.

What can we learn from this deliberate act, the entry of the ultimate King on a humble donkey? We must rethink the very nature of leadership.

On his eightieth birthday, Swiss theologian Karl Barth reframed the story of Jesus riding into Jerusalem on a donkey in a poignant way:

> A real donkey is mentioned in the Bible, or more specifically an ass ... It was permitted to carry Jesus to Jerusalem. If I have done anything in this life of mine, I have done it as a relative of the donkey that went its way carrying an important burden. The disciples had said to its owner: "The Lord has need of it." And so it seems to have pleased God to have used me at this time, just as I was, in spite of all the things, the disagreeable things, that quite rightly are and will be said about me. Thus I was used.[22]

It's not about us. It's not about our glory, our fame, our power, our church buildings, our logo, our branding, our platforms. We're *just the ass*, and we should be honored that God chooses to love us, save us, and that we have the joy of carrying the name and gospel of Christ to our neighborhoods, cities, and world. We shouldn't be riding Jesus for our agenda, because Jesus already has an agenda.

Which Jesus rides in? Or rather, which version of Jesus rides in? More specifically, which Jesus do we prefer? If we're all honest, we have a particular and palatable perspective, angle, identity, and version of Jesus that best fits our lives:

Political Jesus

Republican Jesus

Democrat Jesus

Conservative Jesus

Liberal Jesus

Humanist Jesus

Feminist Jesus

Mixed Martial Arts Jesus

Social Justice Jesus

Revolutionary Jesus

Militant Jesus

Nationalistic Jesus

Homeboy Jesus

Bless Me Jesus

ATM Jesus

Healer Jesus

Black, Brown, Asian, or White, Blond, Blue-Eyed Jesus

In-Case-of-Emergency Jesus

Prosperity, Health, and Wealth Jesus

Poverty Jesus

Fill-in-the-Blank Jesus

The good news is that Jesus is able to speak to each of us and our circumstances. Even more good news is that Jesus can never be contained by the boxes we impose on Him. Which Jesus rode in? For the crowds in Jerusalem, many saw Him and cried out:

> "Hosanna to the Son of David!"
> "Blessed is he who comes in the name of the Lord!"
> "Hosanna in the highest heaven!" (Matt. 21:9)

"Hosanna," now a declaration of praise, was originally a plea for salvation. The people cried out to be saved, but they are a poignant reminder of our human nature. The city gave its heart to Jesus on the first day of the week only to kill Him five days later.

A DIFFERENT KIND OF KING

In two thousand years, little has changed about our nature. We're hedonists, pleasure seekers, ego seekers, and self-seekers. But Jesus Christ—the Lord of Lords, King of Kings, the Morning Star, the Savior of All Humanity—has His own ways, higher than our ways. And His ways are often to lower Himself to become accessible to everyone.

While on earth, Jesus spent precious time with prostitutes, homeless and destitute people, Samaritans, lepers, the powerful, and the powerless. Jesus turned the social norms upside down and engaged women, the poor, Gentiles, and social outcasts of His time. In fact, during those days, people were judged by three major criteria: gender, race, and economics. This is precisely why Paul's declaration in his letter to the church in Galatia was so powerful when he summarized the message and the embodiment of Jesus' ministry:

> There is neither Jew nor Greek, there is neither slave
> nor free, there is neither male nor female; for you are
> all one in Christ Jesus. (Gal. 3:28 NKJV)

Jesus is a different kind of King! His rule is the rule of love, not of coercion and force. It is the rule of sacrifice. His kingdom is unlike any other kind on earth. Jesus entered this world in a time of hostility when the Roman Empire was expanding. Joseph and Mary made the trek to Bethlehem for the census, that we know. But the reason for the census was for taxation, in order to fulfill the agenda of the Pax Romana, the expanding Roman Empire. Caesar demanded a census in order to tax citizens and in turn expand the military.[23]

Jesus arrived on the scene and, even as a baby, threatened the authority of the government. Because of Jesus' birth, King Herod had all boys killed, age two and younger, in the vicinity of Bethlehem.[24] This was genocide. And yet, even as Jesus embodied justice, He still spoke of mercy. He preached to love our neighbors. Jesus won His subjects, not by force or suppression, but by going to die for them on the cross—the greatest, most subversive symbol of victory.

When Jesus entered Jerusalem, He could have rolled in on a chariot, preceded by 250 oxen with horns covered in gold, accompanied by a choir. As Aemilius wore a purple robe on his way into Rome, Jesus also was clothed in a purple robe. Except Jesus wore it when He was led away by His executioners.[25] They also put a crown on His head when they hailed Him as king. A crown of thorns.

He is not the King who asks what you can do for your country; He is the King who does for you what you could never do for yourself. He gave His life for you. Jesus, the humble King on a donkey, Savior of all who believe. Through His sacrifice, we have a perfect example of how to live, and we have a future. We know how this story will end, because regardless of who is in power, our King will prevail.

WHAT'S ON YOUR HEART AND MIND?

1. Since Jesus remains King over all, what should our approach toward politics be?

2. How should we draw the line between faith and responsibility as global citizens?

3. Clearly, your faith should inform your voting. But how does your faith inform your actions and attitudes toward those who don't vote like you do?

THOU SHALT NOT FEAR

Before any worldly ideology, we must first place our hope in Christ. He is our rock and fortress, the solid ground on which we can stand, despite our human questions and uncertainties. Jesus is Lord, not the ideology or the leader of the moment. We have something with more significance than any ideology, something more significant than the outcome of any election.

Hope came not in the form of a politician, political party or system, or great nation. Rather, hope arrived in the person of Jesus Christ. He came in the most unusual and unexpected way, in a form that confused even those closest to Him, even up to His death. Jesus did not show up as a royal king with pomp and power, but one who humbled Himself in every way. He came to earth to teach, challenge, love, and fulfill ancient prophecy in a way far more significant than anyone expected. Remember, He came to seek the lost, the last, and the least, and to invite people to join Him. He came to save sinners like you and me and to make reconciliation possible with God and with one another. He came to redeem humanity, to offer hope for all.

Hope arrived, and it was so much better than we could ever dream.

Hope arrived … and thank God it did.

Remember this, Christian:

"Whoever becomes President, Jesus remains King."

I don't know who to attribute this quote to as I've seen it in several places, but it captures the Truth that even in the midst of chaos, God remains sovereign. While some may grow nervous at the mention of God's sovereignty, don't misunderstand its meaning. God's sovereignty should not be interpreted that God causes everything but, rather, that God is able to do anything. I once heard a theology professor share that "everything that happens is within God's will, but God doesn't will everything that happens."

The earth may shake, mountains may fall, disasters may come, and leaders we like or do not like may come into power, but Jesus remains King. God remains in control. Regardless of any temporal circumstance, Jesus is Lord. He is who He says He is, and He will accomplish what He says He will accomplish. And Jesus will return one day to restore all things unto Himself. Until then, we are invited to participate in His glorious work in a broken and messy world.

When we place our identity and faith in the poll-informed political leaders of our land, we are selling ourselves short. Politics do matter, but politics are not the most important thing in life. It is far more important to believe that Jesus is Lord—and for that belief to transform and inform the way we embody our lives as followers of Christ.

Amid the craziness of our world—past, present, and future—we believe in a Savior who entered human creation as a baby and grew up to be the ultimate teacher and ultimate sacrifice. That does not change when the other party wins. That does not change when the legislation you are advocating for does not go through.

Everyone, take a breath. Breathe in. Breathe out. Political leaders come, and political leaders go, but through every election, through every year, every century, every millennium, Jesus remains King.

Many of our political opinions and choices have been based in fear. But the Holy Scriptures remind us in 2 Timothy 1:7: "For God has not given us a spirit of fear, but of power and of love and of a sound mind."[1] When we trust in God's power and act in love, there is nothing to fear.

While *Thou Shalt Not Be a Jerk* is a good book title and good life advice, we should consider it as a minimum standard. It is easier to understand the Golden Rule, "Do unto others as you would have them do unto you." It seems logical. It's a way of behaving that might be challenging, but we understand it. People treat you well; treat them well in return. Compare that with the greatest commandments as proclaimed by Jesus, to love God and love our neighbors. Full stop. No matter what, we should love. A broad, all-encompassing way to live.

As Christ followers, let's not only not be jerks, but let's espouse the love of Christ for our neighbors at all times, for everyone, everywhere. After all, "there is no fear in love. But perfect love drives out fear."[2]

Earthly kings, presidents, congressmen, and senators will come and go, but Jesus is the eternal King. No matter who is in power, our lives are in His hands. This doesn't guarantee bliss and perfection. We'll all certainly face challenges and difficulties, but our lives still remain in His hands. We have to remind ourselves and others that Jesus ultimately defeated sin and death. We can declare to all who have ears to hear the good news that through Jesus, a new world is breaking forth amid the brokenness. When we truly believe this, there's no need to be a jerk.

Jesus will always remain on His throne. Amen and amen.

NOTES

Introduction: Politics Matter

1. Sean Illing, "What's Wrong with America? I Debate Ben Shapiro," Vox, May 9, 2019, www.vox.com/2019/5/9/18410886/ben-shapiro-right-side-of-history.

2. Christine Schliesser, "From 'a Theology of Genocide' to a 'Theology of Reconciliation'? On the Role of Christian Churches in the Nexus of Religion and Genocide in Rwanda," 2018, MDPI, https://doi.org/10.3390/rel9020034.

3. Peter Gwin, "Revisiting the Rwandan Genocide: How Churches Became Death Traps," *National Geographic*, April 2, 2014, www.nationalgeographic.com /photography/proof/2014/04/02/revisiting-the-rwandan-genocide-how -churches-became-death-traps/.

4. Camila Domonoske, "A Boatload of Ballots: Midterm Voter Turnout Hit 50-Year High," NPR, November 8, 2018, www.npr.org/2018/11/08 /665197690/a-boatload-of-ballots-midterm-voter-turnout-hit-50-year-high.

5. John Howard Griffin, *Follow the Ecstasy: The Hermitage Years of Thomas Merton* (Maryknoll, NY: Orbis Books, 1993), 112.

Chapter 1: Thou Shalt Not Go to Bed with Political Parties

1. "Here's How Seattle Voters' Support for Trump Compared to Other Cities'," *Seattle Times*, November 17, 2019, www.seattletimes.com/seattle-news/politics /heres-how-seattle-voters-support-for-trump-stacks-up-to-other-u-s-cities/.

2. Kim Parker, Nikki Graf, and Ruth Igielnik, "Generation Z Looks a Lot Like Millennials on Key Social and Political Issues," Pew Research Center, January

17, 2019, www.pewsocialtrends.org/2019/01/17/generation-z-looks-a-lot-like -millennials-on-key-social-and-political-issues/.

3. Ben Tappin, Leslie Van Der Leer, and Ryan Mckay, "You're Not Going to Change Your Mind," *New York Times*, May 27, 2019, www.nytimes.com/2017/05/27 /opinion/sunday/youre-not-going-to-change-your-mind.html.

4. "Trump in 1999: 'I Am Very Pro-Choice'" video, NBC News, posted July 8, 2015, www.nbcnews.com/meet-the-press/video/trump-in-1999-i-am-very -pro-choice-480297539914.

5. Katharine Jackson, "Trump Tells Anti-Abortion Marchers He Will Support Them," Reuters, January 18, 2019, www.reuters.com/article/us-usa-abortion /trump-tells-anti-abortion-marchers-he-will-support-them-idUSKCN1PC215.

6. Joel Roberts, "Kerry's Top Ten Flip-Flops," CBS News, September 29, 2004, www.cbsnews.com/news/kerrys-top-ten-flip-flops/.

7. Lily Rothman, "The Story behind Bill Clinton's Infamous Denial," *Time*, January 26, 2015, http://time.com/3677042/clinton-lewinsky-response/.

8. Alec Tyson, "The 2018 Midterm Vote: Divisions by Race, Gender, Education," Pew Research Center, November 8, 2018, www.pewresearch.org/fact-tank /2018/11/08/the-2018-midterm-vote-divisions-by-race-gender-education/.

9. "Democratic Party," Encyclopaedia Britannica, July 17, 2019, www.britannica .com/topic/Democratic-Party#ref797856.

10. Michael Nelson, "How Vietnam Broke the Democratic Party," *New York Times*, March 28, 2018, www.nytimes.com/2018/03/28/opinion/vietnam-broke -democratic-party.html.

11. Nelson, "How Vietnam," www.nytimes.com/2018/03/28/opinion/vietnam -broke-democratic-party.html.

12. Jane C. Timm, "Trump on Hot Mic: 'When You're a Star … You Can Do Anything' to Women," NBC News, October 7, 2016, www.nbcnews.com /politics/2016-election/trump-hot-mic-when-you-re-star-you-can-do-n662116.

13. Amber Phillips, "'They're Rapists.' President Trump's Campaign Launch Speech Two Years Later, Annotated," *Washington Post*, June 16, 2017, www.washingtonpost.com/news/the-fix/wp/2017/06/16/theyre-rapists -presidents-trump-campaign-launch-speech-two-years-later-annotated/?utm _term=.6da0a25152b3.

14. Michael Gerson, "The Last Temptation," *Atlantic*, April 2018, www.theatlantic .com/magazine/archive/2018/04/the-last-temptation/554066/.

15. Franklin Graham, "Clinton's Sins Aren't Private," *Wall Street Journal*, August 27, 1998, www.wsj.com/articles/SB904162265981632000.

16. Eliza Griswold, "Franklin Graham's Uneasy Alliance with Donald Trump," September 11, 2018, *New Yorker*, https://www.newyorker.com/news/dispatch /franklin-grahams-uneasy-alliance-with-donald-trump.

17. "Franklin Graham: Trump 'Defends the Faith,'" Axios, November 26, 2018, www.axios.com/franklin-graham-donald-trump-6b18159f-d481-48e2-9eb3 -ea48f4eb26aa.html.

18. John Fea, "What James Dobson Said in 1998 about Moral Character and the Presidency," *Way of Improvement Leads Home* (blog), June 25, 2016, https://thewayofimprovement.com/2016/06/25/james-dobson-on-the -character-of-the-president-of-the-united-states/.

19. "Dr. James Dobson on Donald Trump's Christian Faith," Dr. James Dobson's Family Talk, accessed October 8, 2019, http://drjamesdobson.org/news/dr -james-dobson-on-trumps-christian-faith.

20. Michael Wear, *Reclaiming Hope: Lessons Learned in the Obama White House about the Future of Faith in America* (Nashville, TN: Thomas Nelson Books), xxix.

21. Diana Butler Bass, *A People's History of Christianity: The Other Side of the Story* (New York: HarperOne, 2009), 80–81.

22. I agree with Michael Wear's thoughts on this topic. See his March 28, 2017, tweet: https://twitter.com/MichaelRWear/status/846912054162264064.

Chapter 2: Thou Shalt Not Be a Jerk

1. Eugene Peterson (quoted by @PetersonDaily), Twitter, February 3, 2015, 6:49 p.m., https://twitter.com/PetersonDaily/status/562805039597895681.

2. Russell Moore, *Onward: Engaging the Culture without Losing the Gospel* (Nashville, TN: B&H Publishing Group, 2015), dust jacket and 82.

3. "A List of Some of the More Than #2000Verses in Scripture on Poverty and Justice," Sojourners, accessed October 8, 2019, https://sojo.net/list-some -more-2000verses-scripture-poverty-and-justice.

4. David Kinnaman and Gabe Lyons, *Unchristian: What a Generation Really Thinks about Christianity … and Why It Matters* (Grand Rapids, MI: Baker Books, 2007), 29–30.

5. Shane Claiborne, "Evangelicalism Must Be Born Again," chapter 9 in Mark Labberton, ed., *Still Evangelical? Insiders Reconsider Political, Social, and Theological Meaning* (Downers Grove, IL: InterVarsity, 2018), 153–54.

6. Douglas L. Mendenhall, "Comparing Levels of Incivility across Religious and Political Blog Posts," PhD dissertation, Texas Tech University, 2014.

7. Sarah Sobieraj, "Patterned Resistance to Women's Visibility in Digital Publics, Information, Communication and Society," 2018, 21:11, 1700-1714, DOI: 10.1080/1369118X.2017.1348535.

8. "Troll Patrol Findings: Using Crowdsourcing, Data Science and Machine Learning to Measure Violence and Abuse against Women on Twitter," Amnesty International, accessed June 15, 2019, https://decoders.amnesty.org /projects/troll-patrol/findings#what_did_we_find_container.

9. Justin Cheng, Cristian Danescu-Niculescu-Mizil, and Michael Bernstein, "Why People Troll, according to Science," Business Insider, March 2, 2017, www.businessinsider.com/find-out-why-any-of-us-are-capable-of-trolling-2017-3.

10. Ephrat Livni, "A Stanford Psychologist Says Internet Culture Isn't as Toxic as It Feels," Quartz, August, 19, 2017, https://qz.com/1055662/a-stanford -psychologist-says-internet-culture-isnt-as-toxic-as-it-feels/.

11. Livni, "Stanford Psychologist," https://qz.com/1055662/a-stanford-psychologist -says-internet-culture-isnt-as-toxic-as-it-feels/.

12. Aaron Smith, "Declining Majority of Online Adults Say the Internet Has Been Good for Society," Pew Research Center, April 30, 2018, www.pewinternet .org/2018/04/30/declining-majority-of-online-adults-say-the-internet-has -been-good-for-society/.

13. Daniel Cox, Juhem Navarro-Rivera, and Robert P. Jones, "Race, Religion, and Political Affiliation of Americans' Core Social Networks," Public Religion Research Institute, August 3, 2016, www.prri.org/research/poll-race-religion -politics-americans-social-networks/.

14. Christopher Ingraham, "Three Quarters of Whites Don't Have Any Non-White Friends," *Washington Post*, August 25, 2014, www.washingtonpost.com/news /wonk/wp/2014/08/25/three-quarters-of-whites-dont-have-any-non -white-friends/.

15. Psalm 139:14.

Chapter 3: Thou Shalt Listen and Build Bridges

1. "Clinton: Half of Trump Supporters 'Basket of Deplorables,'" BBC, September 10, 2016, www.bbc.com/news/av/election-us-2016-37329812/clinton-half-of-trump-supporters-basket-of-deplorables.

2. Dylan Matthews, "We Shouldn't Have to Explain That Ted Cruz's Dad Didn't Kill JFK, but Here Goes, I Guess," Vox, May 3, 2016, www.vox.com/2016/5/3/11580740/ted-cruz-lee-harvey-oswald-donald-trump.

3. Bianca Taylor, "At 'Make America Dinner Again,' Bridging Political and Racial Divides," KQED, September 23, 2017, www.kqed.org/news/11618110/at-make-america-dinner-again-bridging-political-and-racial-divides.

4. Make America Dinner Again, Facebook post, April 1, 2019, accessed June 15, 2019, www.facebook.com/makeamericadinneragain/.

5. The Blaze, Facebook video post, April 26, 2018, accessed June 15, 2019, www.facebook.com/theblaze/videos/18297440067062925/.

6. "Glenn Beck Original Clip on Social Justice and Churches from March 2, 2010," Right Scoop YouTube channel, posted March 15, 2010, www.youtube.com/watch?v=5c4DqdleJuY.

7. Jenna Johnson, "Trump Calls for 'Total and Complete Shutdown of Muslims Entering the United States,'" Washington Post, December 7, 2015, www.washingtonpost.com/news/post-politics/wp/2015/12/07/donald-trump-calls-for-total-and-complete-shutdown-of-muslims-entering-the-united-states/?utm_term=.ee94e61f672a.

8. "Muslims," Pew Research Center, accessed October 9, 2019, www.pewforum.org/religious-landscape-study/religious-tradition/muslim/.

9. "Ask A ...," KUOW, May 5, 2017, www.kuow.org/series/ask.

10. Jim Daly, "The Importance of Listening in Today's Evangelicalism," chapter 10 in Mark Labberton, ed., Still Evangelical? Insiders Reconsider Political, Social, and Theological Meaning (Downers Grove, IL: InterVarsity, 2018), 179.

11. "Our Story: Depolarize America, from South Lebanon, Ohio, to All Fifty States," Better Angels, accessed October 9, 2019, www.better-angels.org/our-story/#leadership.

Chapter 4: Thou Shalt Be about the Kingdom of God

1. Matthew 11:3.

2. Matthew 4:17.

3. Mark 10:14.

4. John 16:33.

5. Marcus J. Borg, "Jesus and Politics," Bible Odyssey, accessed October 9, 2019, www.bibleodyssey.org/en/people/related-articles/jesus-and-politics.

6. Rick McKinley, *This Beautiful Mess* (Colorado Springs: Multnomah Books, 2006), 56–57.

7. 1 Peter 2:9 KJV.

8. Timothy Keller, "How Do Christians Fit into the Two-Party System? They Don't," *New York Times*, September 29, 2018, www.nytimes.com/2018/09/29/opinion/sunday/christians-politics-belief.html.

9. Michael Wear, *Reclaiming Hope: Lessons Learned in the Obama White House about the Future of Faith in America* (Nashville, TN: Thomas Nelson Books), 226.

10. Keller, "How Do Christians Fit," www.nytimes.com/2018/09/29/opinion/sunday/christians-politics-belief.html.

11. "Abortion Is a Common Experience for U.S. Women, Despite Dramatic Declines in Rates," Guttmacher Institute, October 19, 2017, www.guttmacher.org/news-release/2017/abortion-common-experience-us-women-despite-dramatic-declines-rates.

12. Nicole Brodeur, "How 'Shout Your Abortion' Grew from a Seattle Hashtag into a Book," *Seattle Times*, December 13, 2018, www.seattletimes.com/life/how-shout-your-abortion-grew-from-a-seattle-hashtag-into-a-book/.

13. Keith Giles, "The Shiny Red Button (How Republicans Use Abortion to Manipulate Christians)," Patheos, January 28, 2019, www.patheos.com/blogs/keithgiles/2019/01/the-shiny-red-button-how-republicans-use-abortion-to-manipulate-christians/.

14. Jim Daly, "The Importance of Listening in Today's Evangelicalism," chapter 10 in Mark Labberton, ed., *Still Evangelical? Insiders Reconsider Political, Social, and Theological Meaning* (Downers Grove, IL: InterVarsity, 2018), 179.

15. "Abortion Is a Common Experience," Guttmacher, www.guttmacher.org/news-release/2017/abortion-common-experience-us-women-despite-dramatic-declines-rates.

16. Linda Carroll, "LGBT Youth at Higher Risk for Suicide Attempts," Reuters, October 8, 2018, www.reuters.com/article/us-health-lgbt-teen-suicide/lgbt-youth-at-higher-risk-for-suicide-attempts-idUSKCN1MI1SL.

17. "Abortion Is Increasingly Concentrated among Poor Women," Guttmacher Institute, October 19, 2017, www.guttmacher.org/infographic/2017/abortion-rates-income.

18. Nat Levy, "Seattle Median Home Price Hits Record $820K, Soaring $43K in a Month, Putting Buyers in a 'Pressure Cooker,'" GeekWire, April 6, 2018, www.geekwire.com/2018/seattle-median-home-price-hits-record-820k-soaring-43k-month-putting-buyers-pressure-cooker/.

19. "Count Us In Shows Significant Reduction in Veteran Homelessness, Small Overall Increase in Homelessness for Seattle/King County," All Home, May 31, 2018, http://allhomekc.org/wp-content/uploads/2018/06/Count-Us-In-2018-news-release-5.31.pdf.

20. Kate Walters, "Seattle Homeless Population Is Third Largest in U.S., after LA and NYC," KUOW, December 18, 2018, www.kuow.org/stories/here-s-how-seattle-and-washington-compare-to-national-homeless-trends.

Chapter 5: Thou Shalt Live Out Your Convictions

1. Deanna Weniger, "Bartz Brothers of New Brighton's Latest Snow Sculpture: A Silly, Surprised Snail," *Twin Cities Pioneer Press*, January 3, 2019, www.twincities.com/2019/01/01/bartz-brothers-of-new-brighton-unveil-eighth-snow-sculpture-on-new-years-day/.

2. "Leo Tolstoy's Infamous Quote: 'No One Thinks of Changing Himself,'" posted by Andrea Schlottman, Books on the Wall, accessed October 10, 2019, https://booksonthewall.com/blog/leo-tolstoy-quote/.

3. "Dietrich Bonhoeffer Biography," Biography Online, March 8, 2017, www.biographyonline.net/spiritual/dietrich-bonhoeffer.html; and Janie B. Cheaney, "Man in Conflict," *World Magazine*, February 14, 2019, https://world.wng.org/2019/02/man_in_conflict.

4. E. Forrest Harris Sr., "The Black Church's Influence on Dietrich Bonhoeffer," *Bonhoeffer Blog*, February 21, 2009, https://bonhoefferblog.wordpress.com/2009/02/21/the-black-churchs-influence-on-dietrich-bonhoeffer/.

5. Bree Newsome, "Shake It Like an Etch-A-Sketch!," Vimeo, September 8, 2012, https://vimeo.com/49088272.

6. Jason Hanna and Ralph Ellis, "Confederate Flag's Half-Century at South Carolina Capitol Ends," CNN, July 10, 2015, www.cnn.com/2015/07/10/us/south-carolina-confederate-battle-flag/index.html.

7. Lottie Joiner, "Bree Newsome Reflects on Taking Down South Carolina's Confederate Flag 2 Years Ago," Vox, June 27, 2017, www.vox.com/identities /2017/6/27/15880052/bree-newsome-south-carolinas-confederate-flag.

8. Megan Rivers (@MegMRivers), "Suspect in #CharlestonChurchShooting caught in Shelby, NC. He's believed to have killed 9 ppl last night at a church," Twitter, June 18, 2015, 8:14 a.m., https://twitter.com/MegMRivers /status/611552652896436224.

9. Matt Zapotosky, "Charleston Church Shooter: 'I Would Like to Make It Crystal Clear, I Do Not Regret What I Did,'" *Washington Post*, January 4, 2017, www.washingtonpost.com/world/national-security/charleston-church-shooter -i-would-like-to-make-it-crystal-clear-i-do-not-regret-what-i-did/2017/01/04 /05b0061e-d1da-11e6-a783-cd3fa950f2fd_story.html?utm_term=.de6bb2165d81.

10. Joiner, "Bree Newsome Reflects," www.vox.com/identities/2017/6/27 /15880052/bree-newsome-south-carolinas-confederate-flag.

11. Hanna and Ellis, "Confederate Flag's Half-Century," www.cnn.com/2015 /07/10/us/south-carolina-confederate-battle-flag/index.html.

12. "Mission," Refresh Conference, accessed October 10, 2019, https://therefreshconference.org/our-mission/.

13. "Why Family Reunification?," 1MillionHome, accessed October 10, 2019, https://1millionhome.com/why-family-reunification/.

14. Katayoun Kishi, "Assaults against Muslims in U.S. Surpass 2001 Level," Pew Research Center, November 15, 2017, www.pewresearch.org/fact-tank /2017/11/15/assaults-against-muslims-in-u-s-surpass-2001-level/.

15. "Andrew Larsen—Visual Peacemaking, Extended Version, September 2013," posted by John Yeager, Vimeo, September 6, 2013, https://vimeo.com /73943630.

16. Matthew 5:9.

Chapter 6: Thou Shalt Have Perspective and Depth

1. James C. Cobb, "Even Though He Is Revered Today, MLK Was Widely Disliked by the American Public When He Was Killed," Smithsonian.com, April 4, 2018, www.smithsonianmag.com/history/why-martin-luther-king -had-75-percent-disapproval-rating-year-he-died-180968664/.

2. Martin Luther King Jr., "Quotable Quote," Goodreads, accessed October 10, 2019, www.goodreads.com/quotes/943-darkness-cannot-drive-out-darkness -only-light-can-do-that; www.goodreads.com/quotes/6407-our-lives-begin -to-end-the-day-we-become-silent; and www.goodreads.com/quotes/16312 -faith-is-taking-the-first-step-even-when-you-can-t.

3. "RNC Message Celebrating Martin Luther King Jr. Day," Republican National Committee, accessed June 16, 2019, www.gop.com/rnc-message-celebrating -martin-luther-king-jr-day/?.

4. "DNC on Dr. Martin Luther King Jr. Day," Democratic National Committee, January 21, 2019, https://democrats.org/news/dnc-on-dr-martin-luther -king-jr-day/.

5. Michelle Garcia, "Ram Uses Martin Luther King's Anticapitalist Sermon to Sell Pickup Trucks," Vox, February 5, 2018, www.vox.com/2018/2/4/16972220 /martin-luther-king-dodge-ram-super-bowl-ad.

6. Adam Serwer, "Lyndon Johnson Was a Civil Rights Hero. But Also a Racist," MSNBC, April 12, 2014, www.msnbc.com/msnbc/lyndon-johnson-civil -rights-racism.

7. Vann R. Newkirk II, "The Consequences of Martin Luther King Jr.'s Canonization," *Atlantic*, January 21, 2019, www.theatlantic.com/politics/archive/2019/01/martin -luther-kings-legacy-and-those-who-claim-it/580903/.

8. Garcia, "Ram Uses Martin Luther King's Anticapitalist Sermon," www.vox.com /2018/2/4/16972220/martin-luther-king-dodge-ram-super-bowl-ad.

9. Diana Butler Bass, *A People's History of Christianity: The Other Side of the Story* (New York: HarperOne, 2009), 5.

10. Bass, *People's History*, 5.

11. Luke 10:37.

12. Mark 8:36.

13. Kate Shellnutt, "Hong Kong Pastor Facing Prison Preaches the Sermon of His Life," *Christianity Today*, April 10, 2019, www.christianitytoday.com/news /2019/april/hong-kong-pastor-occupy-umbrella-movement-chu-yiu-ming .html; and Matthew 5:10.

14. "Persecuted and Forgotten? A Report on Christians Oppressed for Their Faith 2015–17 Executive Summary," Aid to the Church in Need, accessed October 11, 2019, www.churchinneed.org/wp-content/uploads/2017/10/persecution -1-1.pdf, 10.

15. "About the Ranking: How the Scoring Works," Open Doors, accessed October 11, 2019, www.opendoorsusa.org/christian-persecution/world-watch -list/about-the-ranking/.

16. "North Korea," Open Doors, accessed October 11, 2019, www.opendoorsusa .org/christian-persecution/world-watch-list/north-korea/.

17. "Persecuted and Forgotten?," Aid to the Church in Need, www.churchinneed .org/wp-content/uploads/2017/10/persecution-1-1.pdf, 5.

18. Jeff Sessions, "Attorney General Sessions Addresses Recent Criticisms of Zero Tolerance by Church Leaders," United States Department of Justice, June 14, 2018, www.justice.gov/opa/speech/attorney-general-sessions-addresses-recent -criticisms-zero-tolerance-church-leaders.

19. T. L. Carter, "The Irony of Romans 13," 2004, *Novum Testamentum* 46 (3): 209.

20. Matthew 22:21.

21. "Harriet Beecher Stowe: Author of *Uncle Tom's Cabin*," *Christianity Today*, accessed October 11, 2019, www.christianitytoday.com/history/people /musiciansartistsandwriters/harriet-beecher-stowe.html.

22. "A Conversation with Nancy Koester on Harriet Beecher Stowe," video, *Eerdword* (blog), June 30, 2014, https://eerdword.com/2014/06/30/a -conversation-with-nancy-koester-on-harriet-beecher-stowe/.

23. Inyoung Kang, "Overlooked No More: Yu Gwan-sun, a Korean Independence Activist Who Defied Japanese Rule," *New York Times*, March 28, 2018, www.nytimes.com/2018/03/28/obituaries/overlooked-yu-gwan-sun.html.

24. "Yu Gwan-sun," New World Encyclopedia, accessed October 11, 2019, www.newworldencyclopedia.org/entry/Yu_Gwansun.

25. Kang, "Overlooked No More," www.nytimes.com/2018/03/28/obituaries /overlooked-yu-gwan-sun.html.

26. "Compare the Two Speeches," Sojourner Truth Project, accessed October 11, 2019, www.thesojournertruthproject.com/compare-the-speeches/. *Note: Two versions of Truth's famous speech are widely circulated. This excerpt is from the version published by Marius Robinson in the* Anti-Slavery Bugle *less than a month after it was delivered on May 29, 1851.*

27. Christopher Metress, "Literary Representations of the Lynching of Emmett Till: An Annotated Bibliography," *Emmett Till in Literary Memory and Imagination*, ed. Harriet Pollack and Christopher Metress (Baton Rouge, LA: Louisiana State UP, 2008), 223–50, cited in Harold K. Bush, "Continuing Bonds and Emmett Till's Mother," *Southern Quarterly* 50, no. 3 (Spring 2013): 9–27.

Chapter 7: Thou Shalt Not Lie, Get Played, or Be Manipulated

1. John Blake, "The Viral Presidency: Obama's Best Unscripted Moments," CNN, May 20, 2015, https://edition.cnn.com/2015/05/20/politics/viral-presidency -obama-unscripted-moments/index.html.

2. Frank James, "Photo of Romney's 'Shoe Shine' Actually Shows Security Check," NPR, January 12, 2012, www.npr.org/sections/itsallpolitics/2012/01/12 /145126797/photo-of-romneys-shoe-shine-actually-shows-security-check.

3. Kaya Taitano, "Teenagers Taunt Native American Elder in Washington," video, *New York Times*, October 12, 2019, www.nytimes.com/video/us /100000006316066/teenagers-maga-native-american-video.html.

4. "Students in 'MAGA' Hats Taunt Indigenous Elder, Demonstrators in Washington: VIDEO," WLS-TV, January 21, 2019, https://abc7chicago.com/politics /boys-in-maga-hats-mock-indigenous-elder-in-dc-video/5097427/.

5. Max Londberg, "'Blatant Racism': Kentucky High School Apologizes Following Backlash after Video Shows Students Surrounding Indigenous Marchers," *USA Today*, January 24, 2019, www.usatoday.com/story/news/nation /2019/01/19/kentucky-diocese-incident-indigenous-peoples-march -covington-catholic-high-school/2624503002/.

6. Ray Sanchez and Carma Hassan, "Report Finds No Evidence of 'Offensive or Racist Statements' by Kentucky Students," CNN, March 12, 2019, https://edition.cnn.com/2019/02/13/us/covington-catholic-high-school -report/index.html.

7. Tom McKay, "Congress Now Wants Twitter to Explain How the Covington Teens Video Went Viral," Gizmodo, January 22, 2019, https://gizmodo.com /congress-now-wants-twitter-to-explain-how-that-covingto-1831971692.

8. Katy Steinmetz, "How Your Brain Tricks You into Believing Fake News," *Time*, August 9, 2018, http://time.com/5362183/the-real-fake-news-crisis/.

9. Steinmetz, "How Your Brain," http://time.com/5362183/the-real-fake-news-crisis/.

10. Ed Pilkington, "How the Drudge Report Ushered in the Age of Trump," *Guardian*, January 24, 2018, www.theguardian.com/us-news/2018/jan/24 /how-the-drudge-report-ushered-in-the-age-of-trump.

11. Henry Blodget, "It's Time People Realized That the Drudge Report Is a Major Media Property Worth Hundreds of Millions of Dollars," Business Insider, October 10, 2012, www.businessinsider.com/drudge-report-is-worth-2012-10.

12. Hadas Gold, "More Than Two Decades Old, the Drudge Report Hits a New Traffic High," Politico, August 5, 2016, www.politico.com/blogs/on-media /2016/08/more-than-two-decades-old-the-drudge-report-hits-a-new-traffic -high-227008.

13. David Carr and Tim Arango, "A Fox Chief at the Pinnacle of Media and Politics," *New York Times*, January 9, 2010, www.nytimes.com/2010/01/10 /business/media/10ailes.html?pagewanted=1&hp.

14. Henry Blodget, "Fox News Makes More Money Than CNN, MSNBC, and NBC-ABC-and-CBS News Combined," Business Insider, January 10, 2010, www.businessinsider.com/henry-blodget-fox-newss-700-million-man-2010-1.

15. Jonathan Mahler and Jim Rutenberg, "How Rupert Murdoch's Empire of Influence Remade the World," *New York Times*, April 3, 2019, www.nytimes .com/interactive/2019/04/03/magazine/rupert-murdoch-fox-news-trump .html?smid=tw-nytimes&smtyp=cur.

16. Tim Marcin, "Fox News Host Tucker Carlson Reiterates Claim Immigrants Make America Poorer and Dirtier' Even as Advertisers Flee," *Newsweek*, December 18, 2018, www.newsweek.com/fox-news-tucker-carlson-reiterates -immigrants-poorer-dirtier-advertisers-flee-1263765.

17. Chris Ariens, "Here's How Much Ad Revenue the Cable Networks Bring In from Their Biggest Advertisers," TV Newser, April 4, 2018, www.adweek .com/tvnewser/heres-how-much-ad-revenue-the-cable-networks-bring-in -from-their-biggest-advertisers/361164/.

18. Jonathan Mahler, "CNN Had a Problem. Donald Trump Solved It," *New York Times*, April 4, 2017, www.nytimes.com/2017/04/04/magazine/cnn-had-a -problem-donald-trump-solved-it.html.

19. Jessie Newman, "Q&A: Professor Jeffrey Berry Talks about Partisan Politics and Government Shutdowns," *Tufts Daily*, February 5, 2018, https://tuftsdaily .com/features/2018/02/05/q-professor-jeffery-berry-talks-partisan-politics -government-shutdowns/.

20. Alicia Acuna, "Greg Gianforte: Fox News Team Witnesses GOP House Candidate 'Body Slam' Reporter," Fox News, May 25, 2017, www.foxnews .com/politics/greg-gianforte-fox-news-team-witnesses-gop-house-candidate -body-slam-reporter.

21. Dan Mangan, "GOP Rep. Greg Gianforte Wins Re-election in Montana: NBC News," CNBC, November 7, 2018, www.cnbc.com/2018/11/07/gop -rep-greg-gianforte-wins-re-election-in-montana-nbc-news.html.

22. "Statement from President Donald J. Trump on Standing with Saudi Arabia," White House, November 20, 2018, www.whitehouse.gov/briefings-statements/statement-president-donald-j-trump-standing-saudi-arabia/; and Nicole Gaouette and Kaitlan Collins, "Trump Signals US Won't Punish Saudi Crown Prince over Khashoggi Killing," CNN, December 10, 2018, www.cnn.com/2018/11/20/politics/trump-saudi-arabia/index.html.

23. "Trump on Reporters: 'I Hate Some of These People, but I'd Never Kill Them,'" MSNBC, December 22, 2015, www.msnbc.com/msnbc/watch/trump-on-reporters-lying-disgusting-people-589776963857.

24. Claire Fallon, "Where Does the Term 'Fake News' Come From? The 1890s, Apparently," Huffpost, March 24, 2017, www.huffpost.com/entry/where-does-the-term-fake-news-come-from_n_58d53c89e4b03692bea518ad.

25. Sharyl Attkisson, "93 Media Mistakes in the Trump Era: The Definitive List," SharylAttkisson.com, October 5, 2019, https://sharylattkisson.com/2019/01/50-media-mistakes-in-the-trump-era-the-definitive-list/.

26. Glenn Kessler, Salvador Rizzo, and Meg Kelly, "President Trump Has Made 9,014 False or Misleading Claims over 773 Days," *Washington Post*, June 16, 2019, www.washingtonpost.com/politics/2019/03/04/president-trump-has-made-false-or-misleading-claims-over-days/?utm_term=.081c7acc90a0.

27. Matthew Pressman, "Journalistic Objectivity Evolved the Way It Did for a Reason," *Time*, November 5, 2018, http://time.com/5443351/journalism-objectivity-history/.

28. Mike Murphy, "The Most Trusted TV News Brand in the U.S. Isn't Even American," MarketWatch, July 31, 2018, www.marketwatch.com/story/the-most-trusted-tv-news-brand-in-the-us-isnt-even-american-2018-07-31.

29. Indira A. R. Lakshmanan, "Finally Some Good News: Trust in News Is Up, Especially for Local Media," Poynter, August 22, 2018, www.poynter.org/ethics-trust/2018/finally-some-good-news-trust-in-news-is-up-especially-for-local-media/.

30. "2019 Edelman Trust Barometer," Edelman, January 20, 2019, www.edelman.com/trust-barometer.

31. Tom Rosenstiel, "Six Questions That Will Tell You What Media to Trust," American Press Institute, October 22, 2013, www.americanpressinstitute.org/publications/six-critical-questions-can-use-evaluate-media-content/.

32. "Karl Barth," *Christianity Today*, accessed October 12, 2019, www.christianitytoday.com/history/people/theologians/karl-barth.html.

33. "About CBS," Center for Barth Studies at Princeton Theological Seminary, accessed October 12, 2019, http://barth.ptsem.edu/about-cbs/faq.

Chapter 8: Thou Shalt Pray, Vote, and Raise Your Voice

1. David A. Graham, "David Perdue's Prayer for President Obama," *Atlantic*, June 10, 2016, https://www.theatlantic.com/politics/archive/2016/06/david -perdue-obama/486587/.

2. "Will the Southern Baptists Honor Election of Obama?," NPR, June 19, 2009, www.npr.org/templates/story/story.php?storyId=105652770.

3. Francine Kiefer, "Prayer and Politics in Congress," *Christian Science Monitor*, September 17, 2016, www.csmonitor.com/USA/Politics/2016/0917/Prayer -and-politics-in-Congress.

4. Kiefer, "Prayer and Politics," www.csmonitor.com/USA/Politics/2016/0917 /Prayer-and-politics-in-Congress.

5. "Voting Rights Act of 1965," *History*, June 6, 2019, www.history.com/topics /black-history/voting-rights-act.

6. "19th Amendment," *History*, September 9, 2019, www.history.com/topics /womens-history/19th-amendment-1.

7. Becky Little, "Native Americans Weren't Guaranteed the Right to Vote in Every State until 1962," *History*, August 20, 2019, www.history.com/news/native -american-voting-rights-citizenship.

8. Matt Vasilogambros, "Voting Lines Are Shorter—but Mostly for Whites," Pew, February 15, 2018, www.pewtrusts.org/en/research-and-analysis/blogs /stateline/2018/02/15/voting-lines-are-shorter-but-mostly-for-whites.

9. "Voting by Mail and Absentee Voting," MIT Election Data plus Science Lab, accessed October 13, 2019, https://electionlab.mit.edu/research/voting -mail-and-absentee-voting.

10. K. K. Rebecca Lai and Jasmine C. Lee, "Why 10 Percent of Florida Adults Can't Vote: How Felony Convictions Affect Access to the Ballot," *New York Times*, October 6, 2016, www.nytimes.com/interactive/2016/10/06/us /unequal-effect-of-laws-that-block-felons-from-voting.html.

11. Tim Elfrink, "The Long, Racist History of Florida's Now-Repealed Ban on Felons Voting," *Washington Post*, accessed June 16, 2019, www.washingtonpost

.com/nation/2018/11/07/long-racist-history-floridas-now-repealed-ban-felons
-voting/?utm_term=.651b5262399d.

12. "Global Water Crisis: Facts, Faqs, and How to Help," World Vision, accessed
October 13, 2019, www.worldvision.org/clean-water-news-stories/global
-water-crisis-facts.

13. "Under-Five Mortality," World Health Organization, accessed October 13, 2019,
www.who.int/gho/child_health/mortality/mortality_under_five_text/en/.

14. Chris Huber, "Water Facts: Good News and a Global Challenge," World Vision,
April 21, 2017, www.worldvision.org/clean-water-news-stories/water
-facts-good-news-global-challenge.

15. "Water and Sanitation," USAID, May 7, 2019, www.usaid.gov/what-we-do
/water-and-sanitation.

16. Deborah L. Birx, "The United States President's Emergency Plan for AIDS
Relief," US Department of State, accessed October 13, 2019, www.pepfar
.gov/press/releases/282136.htm.

17. John Seven, "What Was George W. Bush's Greatest Achievement?," *History*, May
23, 2018, www.history.com/news/what-was-a-george-w-bushs-greatest
-achievement.

18. "The Very Good Gospel by Lisa Sharon Harper," Red Letter Christians, June 23,
2016, www.redletterchristians.org/books/the-very-good-gospel-by-lisa
-sharon-harper/.

19. "Mother Teresa," Goodreads, accessed October 13, 2019, www.goodreads.com/
quotes/112196-never-worry-about-numbers-help-one-person-at-a-time.

20. Emanuella Grinberg, "Ann Coulter's Backward Use of the R-word," CNN,
October 25, 2012, https://edition.cnn.com/2012/10/23/living/ann-coulter
-obama-tweet/index.html.

21. John Franklin Stephens, "Using the [R-Word] to Describe Me Hurts," *Denver
Post*, September 22, 2016, www.denverpost.com/2008/08/31/using-the-word
-retard-to-describe-me-hurts/.

22. John Franklin Stephens, "Open Letter to Ann Coulter," Special Olympics,
October 23, 2012, https://specialolympicsblog.wordpress.com/2012/10/23
/an-open-letter-to-ann-coulter/. See also "Frank Stephens Takes on Ann Coulter
over Derogatory Term," video, Special Olympics, accessed October 13, 2019,
www.specialolympics.org/stories/news/frank-stephens-takes-on
-ann-coulter-over-derogatory-language.

23. Frank Stephens, testimony before the Subcommittee on Labor, Health and Human Services, and Education, US House of Representatives, October 25, 2017, https://docs.house.gov/meetings/ap/ap07/20171025/106526/hhrg-115 -ap07-wstate-stephensf-20171025.pdf.

24. Jaime L. Natoli, "Prenatal Diagnosis of Down Syndrome: A Systematic Review of Termination Rates (1995–2011)," Obstetrics and Gynaecology, March 14, 2012, https://obgyn.onlinelibrary.wiley.com/doi/full/10.1002/pd.2910.

25. Julian Quinones and Arijeta Lajka, "'What Kind of Society Do You Want to Live In?' Inside the Country Where Down Syndrome Is Disappearing," CBSN On Assignment, August 14, 2017, www.cbsnews.com/news/down-syndrome-iceland/.

26. Quinones and Lajka, "'What Kind of Society,'" www.cbsnews.com/news /down-syndrome-iceland/.

27. "Mr. Fred Rogers Biography: Welcome to His Neighborhood," Biographics, April 10, 2018, https://biographics.org/mr-fred-rogers-biography-welcome -to-his-neighborhood/.

28. Fred Rogers, "Mr. Fred Rogers, Senate Statement on PBS Funding," accessed June 16, 2019, https://americanrhetoric.com/speeches /fredrogerssenatetestimonypbs.htm.

29. Kerri Lawrence, "Celebrating Mr. Rogers at the National Archives," National Archives, March 20, 2019, www.archives.gov/news/articles/celebrating -mr-rogers-at-the-national-archives.

30. Fred Rogers Center, accessed June 16, 2019, https://fredrogerscenter.org.

Chapter 9: Thou Shalt Love God and Love People

1. "Eleanor McCullen," Alliance Defending Freedom, accessed June 16, 2019, www.adflegal.org/detailspages/client-stories-details/eleanor-mccullen.

2. "A Unanimous Supreme Court: Abortion Rights Lose a Buffer," New York Times, June 26, 2014, www.nytimes.com/2014/06/27/opinion/a-unanimous -supreme-court-abortion-rights-lose-a-buffer.html.

3. Liz Hadley, "A Growing Family," World Relief Seattle, accessed October 13, 2019. https://worldreliefseattle.org/blog/growing-family?fbclid =IwAR0eA9VZLnfVtTSOVMqdDlzBvvvyoekEpOBov4xMovEflTkdJuvZdtikSPw.

4. Humanitarian Needs Overview 2019, accessed October 13, 2019, https://hno-syria.org/#key-figures.

5. "Syria Regional Refugee Response," UN High Commissioner for Refugees, accessed October 13, 2019, https://data2.unhcr.org/en/situations/syria/location/71#_ga.

6. "Lebanon: Events of 2018," Human Rights Watch, accessed October 13, 2019, www.hrw.org/world-report/2019/country-chapters/lebanon.

7. John 3:16.

8. See 2 Samuel 3:3.

9. Luke 5:29–30.

10. Luke 19:5 NASB.

11. Dwane Brown, "How One Man Convinced 200 Ku Klux Klan Members to Give Up Their Robes," NPR, August 20, 2017, www.npr.org/2017/08/20 /544861933/how-one-man-convinced-200-ku-klux-klan-members-to-give -up-their-robes.

12. Rachel Chason, "A Black Blues Musician Has a Unique Hobby: Befriending White Supremacists," *Washington Post*, August 30, 2017, www.washingtonpost .com/news/morning-mix/wp/2017/08/30/a-black-blues-musician-has-an -unique-hobby-befriending-white-supremacists/?utm_term=.32a99f58d689.

Chapter 10: Thou Shalt Believe Jesus Remains King

1. Timothy Keller, *The Prodigal Prophet: Jonah and the Mystery of God's Mercy* (New York: Penguin Random House, 2018), 163–64.

2. James Madison, *Federalist No. 51*, 1788.

3. Martin Luther King Jr., "Address at the Religious Leaders Conference on May 11, 1959," Stanford University, accessed October 14, 2019, http://okra .stanford.edu/transcription/document_images/Vol05Scans/11May1959 _AddressattheReligiousLeadersConferenceon11May1959.pdf.

4. Acts 16:25–34.

5. Cathleen Falsani, "Commentary: Nelson Mandela Preached with His Life," Religion News Service, December 10, 2013, https://religionnews.com/2013 /12/10/commentary-nelson-mandela-preached-life/.

6. Jenny Soffel, "5 Ways South Africa Changed after Mandela's Release," World Economic Forum, July 17, 2015, www.weforum.org/agenda/2015/07/5 -ways-south-africa-changed-after-mandelas-release/.

7. Michael Trimmer, "Nelson Mandela and His Faith," Christian Today, December 10, 2013, www.christiantoday.com/article/nelson-mandela-and-his-faith /34956.htm.

8. Matthew 21:1–11; Luke 19:28–38.

9. John 1:46.

10. Matthew 14:8–10.

11. Acts 12:2.

12. "7 Things You Didn't Know about the Apostle Paul," Biblica, October 19, 2018, www.biblica.com/articles/7-things-you-didnt-know-about-the-apostle-paul/.

13. 1 Kings 1:33–44.

14. Sigurd Grindheim, "Your King Is Coming to You," accessed October 14, 2019, www.sigurdgrindheim.com/sermons/king.html.

15. Benjamin Haas, "North Korea Stages Huge Military Parade to Mark 70th Anniversary," *Guardian*, September 9, 2018, www.theguardian.com/world/ 2018/sep/09/north-korea-stages-huge-military-parade-to-mark-70th-anniversary; and Eric Talmadge, "With Military Parade, Kim Jong Un Thumbs Nose at U.S.," *Denver Post*, February 8, 2018, www.denverpost.com/2018/02/08 /north-korea-kim-jong-un-military-parade/.

16. Alix Culbertson, "Bulletproof with a Maximum Speed of 37 MPH—Inside Kim Jong Un's Train," Sky News, March 28, 2018, https://news.sky.com /story/bulletproof-with-a-maximum-speed-of-37mph-inside-kim-jong -uns-train-11307938.

17. Jane Onyanga-Omara, "Guam Missile Launch Plan: Kim Jong Un Waiting for 'Foolish Yankees' Next Move, State Media Reports," CNBC, August 15, 2017, www.cnbc.com/2017/08/15/guam-missile-launch-plan-kim-jong-un -waiting-for-foolish-yankees-next-move-state-media-reports.html.

18. Zachary Cohen, et al., "New Missile Test Shows North Korea Capable of Hitting All of US Mainland," CNN, November 30, 2017, www.cnn .com/2017/11/28/politics/north-korea-missile-launch/index.html; and Associated Press, "North Korea Fires Short-Range Ballistic Missile into Waters off Western Japan," CBC News, May 28, 2017, www.cbc.ca/news /world/north-korea-fire-missile-south-kim-jong-un-1.4135302.

19. "Vladimir Putin Doing Manly Things," CBS News, accessed October 14, 2019, www.cbsnews.com/pictures/vladimir-putin-doing-manly-things/.

20. John Simpson, "Russia's Crimea Plan Detailed, Secret and Successful," BBC, March 19, 2014, www.bbc.com/news/world-europe-26644082.

21. Psalm 20:7 NASB.

22. "Karl Barth's Speech on the Occasion of His Eightieth Birthday Celebrations," in *Fragments Grave and Gay* (London: Collins, 1971), 112–17.

23. Sven Günther, "Taxation in the Greco-Roman World: The Roman Principate," Oxford Handbooks Online, April 2016, DOI: 10.1093/oxfordhb/9780199935390.013.38. See also Alfred Edersheim, "Was There Really a Census When Jesus Was Born?," Christianity.com, accessed June 13, 2019, www.christianity.com/jesus/birth-of-jesus/bethlehem/was-there-really-a-census-at-the-time-of-jesuss-birth.html.

24. Matthew 2:16.

25. Mark 15:17; John 19:2.

Afterword: Thou Shalt Not Fear

1. 2 Timothy 1:7 NKJV.

2. 1 John 4:18.